"Angels have long tors between the Divine and human realms, standing ready to intercede for the benefit of humans. History abounds with accounts of angels coming to the aid of individuals during critical moments, such as during illness and crisis. Joanne Brocas' *The Power of Angel Medicine* will help anyone understand and invoke angelic intercession, and draw closer to the Transcendent."

—Larry Dossey, MD, author of *One Mind*

"Thought I knew a lot about angels, as written my fair share of books about them, but this special book gave me even a fresh perspective. It was a healing and uplifting experience reading it and I know it will be a healing and uplifting experience for all those who read it."

—Theresa Cheung, Sunday Times best-selling author of *An Angel Healed Me*

"My best wishes to the author of this book. I hope it helps the reader to understand to heal sometimes takes more than medicine alone."

—Rev. Colin Fry, Sunday Times best-selling author of *By Your Side*

The
Power
of
Angel
Medicine

Energetic Exercises and Techniques to Activate Divine Healing

JOANNE BROCAS

NEW PAGE BOOKS
A division of The Career Press, Inc.
Pompton Plains, NJ

THE POWER OF ANGEL MEDICINE
EDITED BY JODI BRANDON
TYPESET BY EILEEN MUNSON
Original cover design by Joanna Williams
Printed in the U.S.A.

To order this title, please call toll-free 1-800-CAREER-1 (NJ and Canada: 201-848-0310) to order using VISA or MasterCard, or for further information on books from Career Press.

The Career Press, Inc.
220 West Parkway, Unit 12
Pompton Plains, NJ 07444
www.careerpress.com
www.newpagebooks.com

Library of Congress Cataloging-in-Publication Data

Brocas, Joanne.

The power of angel medicine : energetic exercises and techniques to activate divine healing / by Joanne Brocas. -- 1 [edition].

    pages cm

Includes index.

ISBN 978-1-60163-374-3 -- ISBN 978-1-60163-378-1 (ebook) 1. Spiritual healing. 2. Angels--Miscellanea. I. Title.

BF1999.B677 2015

202'.15--dc23

                                            2015002855

To my

wonderful

husband and earth angel,

Jock Brocas.

Acknowledgments

I would like to express my sincere gratitude to the following people, for without their expert help, support, and guidance, this book would not be available and as perfected as it is today. So thank you very much to:

> › Michael Pye, for saying yes! I am so grateful to Michael for giving this book its wings.

> › Adam Schwartz, for all of his guidance and expertize.

> › Jeff Piasky for the brilliant cover design, which I simply adore.

> › Laurie Pye, who is just delightful, encouraging, and very supportive.

> › The editorial staff, who help my writing style to flow with more ease because I do have a lot to say. *Just listen to me on radio and you will know what I mean.*

> › And to all of the staff at New Page Books/Career Press whom I've not personally met but who play an integral role in the production, admin, and marketing of the book.

Thank you truly from my heart and soul!

Contents

Introduction

Celestial Beings of Divine Light

The Power of Angel Medicine is an extraordinary divine healing book that will help you to explore and discover many simple and all-powerful divine healing exercises and practical energy medicine techniques to help you heal your body, increase your vitality, and co-create your life experience in alignment with a higher power—a divine power. The celestial healing frequencies of God's holy angels can and will help you in all your ways; all you need to do is to open your heart to receive their divine assistance, and follow the easy, step-by-step instructions and guidance outlined within this book just for you. Working with the divine healing energies of the holy angels can help to restore your health when you are sick, console your spirit when you are low, bring a new level of clarity to an anxious mind, and increase your level of joy, creativity, and fulfilment, so that you live your life with a renewed sense of purpose, passion, and spiritual outlook.

Angels are the glorious result of God's creation, just as we humans are the divinely inspired result of God's creation. God created the angels before he created humankind, and therefore the angels are much closer to the divine power and the divine light than we are—closer in terms of frequency and spiritual power, *not distance*. God's divine light holds the most potent, dynamic, and spectacular energy frequency that exists, bar none, within the entire universe. It is the light that emanates directly from the heart and mind of God, containing the holy vibration of divine truth and divine love. Divine light is what sustains and maintains all of creation. Because the angels are closely aligned to the divine power, they serve God by delivering His intercessory works in our life and by acting as holy intermediaries between us and God.

The healing power contained within the divine light of God is so immensely strong that it first needs to be filtered down through the divine assistance of the celestial angels to reach us. Otherwise we could not withstand such powerful healing currents entering directly within our spiritual, energetic, and physical anatomies—*body and soul*. It is these astonishingly powerful divine light frequencies of the celestial angels that I have come to lovingly classify as "angel medicine." And angel medicine *is* divine medicine.

You will discover exactly how the divine light of God, via His holy angels, can personally help to greatly benefit both your health and your life in impressive and numerous ways. Divine light frequencies are truly miraculous and they can especially help you to alter anything in your life that you really do desire to change—health issues, relationship stress, financial stress, career stress, and so forth. The possibilities for such positive change and growth are simply limitless when we willfully and consciously choose to work with the divine light. Here is a quick summary of the fascinating information you will explore within each chapter.

Chapter 1 introduces you to the magnificent holy angels of the divine celestial hierarchy. You will read about the seven majestic Archangels, their divine light frequencies, *the seven emanations of God's consciousness,* and how these incredibly powerful light frequencies can benevolently bless your life. You will also discover spiritual insight about your very own guardian angel, a divine caregiver who carefully watches over your soul. You will be shown how to easily align your mind and consciousness with these wonderful celestial beings, so that you can begin to tap into a source of divine power that is much greater than yourself alone.

Chapter 2 includes important information about your divine spiritual and energetic anatomy so that you can become more familiarized with your own unique energies. You are far more exquisite than just a physical body. You have a beautiful soul and a complex spiritual and energetic anatomy, which consists of a combination of energies ranging in different frequencies. You will discover how to directly work with and positively manipulate your own energies to get your energies running, flowing, and moving in the right directions. This will help to conserve your energy and will help to increase your overall vitality. Looking after your energies in this way will enable you to achieve optimum bodily performance.

Chapter 3 offers you a wonderful mixture of customized angel medicine exercises and energetic techniques to especially help you deal with an array of common health complaints—from headaches and inflammation to general aches and pains. Anyone can use them, as they are easy to apply and learn. These exercises can and will bring you a good level of comfort, which is often instantaneous. They will help to restore the body's vital energy flow, which in turn naturally supports the body's robust health and well-being. And more importantly, they will help to boost the body's immune power to naturally fight off infection and combat illness.

In **Chapter 4** you discover very powerful divine medicine prayer decrees especially formulated to help correct, adjust, and repair old, destructive belief systems that dramatically interfere with your health and happiness. It is through the use of these divine prayers that it is possible to program your energies with new divine beliefs that can completely transform your health and life.

In **Chapter 5**, you are introduced to the fabulous angel healing experts who can help you address those stubborn health issues that continuously persist. You receive divine instruction and perform intricate healing work with these powerful master healers who work with the deeper aspects of divine healing. You discover how the angelic surgeons can utilize the divine light to work deep within your energy field to remove an array of energy anomalies that impact and are directly concerned with significant health issues.

Chapter 6 is all about the fascinating and exciting subject of celestial alchemy. This inspirational chapter reveals exceptionally powerful divine insight into the process of celestial alchemy. You are given very potent, angel medicine–manifesting formulas to help you manifest, co-create, and attract your deepest dreams and heartfelt desires into reality. The holy angels will help you to activate your astonishing creative potential to alter anything in your life that you truly desire to change.

Finally, the **Afterword** rounds off by offering you a superb combination of several angel medicine exercises and energetic techniques especially formulated for you to incorporate into a daily life routine. Not only will this daily routine help you feel more energized, rejuvenated and clear-minded, it will also help you to maintain a healthy energy flow to support your health and to increase the radiant joy of your soul. This daily energetic routine is a wonderful form of preventative medicine, as it will help to keep your energies vibrant and buzzing.

The Power of Angel Medicine will therefore give you the wonderful opportunity to be in greater control of your health, happiness, and life experience. Although the results of divine healing work can be instantaneous and you will often witness signs of immediate improvement, it is still wise to monitor your results over a period of time—and especially so if you have any chronic conditions. Healing changes will always be happening on a spiritual and more subtle energetic level first before they become part of your physical life experience, so stay as patient as you can while you allow this transformational process to happen. Of course, divine healing work can also be miraculous when God's grace and healing power are magnified in our body and life, as many people all around the world have personally testified through their experience of overcoming their medically diagnosed terminal conditions. Divine healing miracles can and do happen.

Using a regular combination of divine healing exercises and energy techniques from this book that you are specifically drawn to will soon bring you fascinating results. Divine healing work is not a substitute for traditional medical care, and you always need to consult a licensed medical practitioner if you are concerned about your health. God's divine healing power can work through any medical practitioner who is especially aligned with the divine. *Angel medicine* can therefore be thought of as a wonderful addition toward wholly improving your health that will work beautifully alongside orthodox medical treatment.

I am more than delighted to bring you the power and knowledge of God's holy angels through this divinely inspired angel medicine healing book. It is truly a one-of-a-kind book due to the clever combination of divine healing exercises and energy medicine techniques. Whatever your request may be to the angels, know that they are always happy to help you in agreement with the will of God for your life. I have had a close personal relationship to the angelic realm ever since I was a small child, when I naturally felt the loving presence of my guardian angel surround me and guide me. Over the years I also began to develop a clear communion to other angelic beings as my soul matured. During my early 20s, I was given a divine message from the angels via a spiritual teacher: that I would eventually write many books for the divine purpose of bringing spiritual knowledge about the angels to the world. This book is part of my destiny that was previously ordained by the celestial angels.

My life with the angels has taught me to trust and rely on God for all of my needs and requirements, while also doing my part through taking any necessary actions and following any divinely inspired opportunities sent to help me. I have always been guided to keep expanding the divine light within my soul. Through my direct experiences with the angels, my continuous research, and my qualifications in energy medicine, and from my knowledge gained by working with thousands of clients and students over the last two decades, I am now able to impart this angelic wisdom and bring this divine healing power straight to you.

My intention in writing this book is to passionately offer you a spiritual approach in which you can gain greater control over your health and your happiness. I should know, because it has certainly helped me, and it can certainly help you. Join me now in Chapter 1, in which you will discover all about the celestial beings of divine light—the magnificent hierarchy of God's holy angels.

Chapter One

The Magnificent Celestial Hierarchy of Angels

*For by Him all things were created: things in heaven
and on earth, visible and invisible, whether thrones or
powers or rulers or authorities; all things were created
by Him and for Him.*

—Colossians 1:16

Angelology is the science and theological study of
angels, and from this study by some of the most influen-
tial experts of Christian theology, such as Saint Thomas
Aquinas (also lovingly known by many as "the Angelic
Doctor"), we can gain the most fascinating knowledge
and divine insight about God's holy angels. Other important angelic research sources include the Bible, The Book
of Enoch, Rudolf Steiner, Emanuel Swedenborg, and
Dionysius's *The Celestial Hierarchy*. The science and study
of angels is extremely important, especially because of the
present craze about angels and the many misconceptions

people have about these holy celestial beings. This chapter will help to shed some divine light on "who's who" in the magnificent celestial hierarchy.

You will come to know about the extraordinary guardian angels and the mighty and majestic Archangels—and their all-powerful divine light frequencies that can help us to heal. I will reveal exactly how you can instantly align your mind with these divine celestial beings through the use of specialized divine prayer decrees. In doing so, you will immediately begin to receive the divine light of God, which will naturally enhance the spiritual power of your soul to help your body heal. You will be tapping into a source of power that is much greater than you alone, and this spiritual process is what activates divine healing. Through receiving the divine light from these glorious celestial beings will also help you to magnify your own spiritual radiance so you can begin to create a happier, more rewarding, and more fulfilling life experience. Divine prayer decrees are instantly activated by an open, loving heart and a sincere belief in a higher power to help you.

Who Are the Angels?

Angels are spiritual beings created by God before God created humankind. God assigned many of these celestial beings different tasks and roles within the universe to help oversee creation. These holy angels are totally devoted to God, and they work in alignment with the will of God and under the direct command of God. God's divine plan created the heavens and the earth—both spirit and matter—which is the formation of the divine spiritual hierarchy. Existing within the divine spiritual hierarchy is the formation of all of God's kingdoms. The angels exist within the glorious celestial kingdom as we human souls exist within the human kingdom.

Within the celestial kingdom the angels are also part of their own structured hierarchy, and this is determined by their species, (guardian angels, archangels, cherubim, principalities, seraphim, and many others) and by their present stage of evolution concerning the spiritual wisdom of their consciousness. Part of the divine plan is for all of God's creations to continuously move heavenward through the eternal spiritual evolution of their individualized consciousness, until God decides to call them home. The magnificent holy angels, who are much closer in vibrational frequency to the divine light of God than we are, can especially help to lovingly guide us in our spiritual evolution and journey as a human soul.

Angels have very refined celestial bodies of spiritual light and are therefore typically unseen and unnoticed by the majority of us when they visit and work within our physical world—which they often do. Only under the direct will and command of God are they able to temporarily appear in physical human form to perform a specific task required of them. This is often known as divine or angelic intervention. There are countless stories worldwide of individuals who claim they were quickly assisted in their hour of need by a mysterious stranger who just as quickly and mysteriously disappeared. Angels don't always need to directly intervene in this way, as they can also influence any humans with light in their soul and who are nearby the person in need, while overlooking the situation and divinely assisting them unseen. This is why humans can, at times of need, shine through for others and be thought of as earth angels.

Angels are assigned many different tasks depending entirely upon the spiritual authority given to them by God. The angels closest in consciousness and vibrational frequency to God are given more spiritual authority and exude more divine power through their presiding over the divine light frequencies. These angels help to maintain all aspects of creation, including the eternal ongoing intricate expansion of God's universe. They have specially assigned roles to work within the cosmos— overseeing the galaxy, the solar system, the planets, the stars, and other important aspects within the heavenly realms. Angels also help to oversee all other life forms and expressions of God's creative energy, both seen and unseen, both spirit and matter.

God's holy angels have very important roles in keeping a careful protective watch over our world of matter.

There are angels who watch over the world's religions. Angels who keep a careful watch over politics and the world's leaders. Angels who watch over the spiritual evolution of each country and nation. Angels who watch over the spiritual evolution of humankind. Angels who look after nature and the seasons. Even angels who prevent the fallen angels from causing mayhem and destruction on earth. You may be wondering why there are constant wars and evil terrorists who attempt to destroy and control humanity when we have so many wonderful divine watchers.

Each person, each country, and each race, along with the earth and all of her inhabitants, are all involved in different stages and degrees of continuous evolution. God does not interfere in these stages of evolution due to the free will He gave us, and due to His divine laws governing evolution. God's holy angels are always in the process of delivering the divine light frequencies to the earth. These powerful divine frequencies filter through the atmosphere of the earth to help clear and diminish the collective and accumulated negative mass of destructive energies created from humanities fear, ignorance, and hatred.

The fallen angels thrive on these destructive energies and draw their power from the world's fear and hatred so they can spread more pain, fear, and hatred on earth. They do not have a separate power from God because there is only the *one* divine power. They have turned away from the one divine power for their own misguided and selfish desires. The divine light of God will always prevail and will constantly weaken their efforts to cause mayhem among us. When we pray for world peace, God's holy angels will immediately adhere to our prayers by directing the divine light frequencies to where we have specifically requested their powerful divine service. It is important to pray for the entire world to be bathed in the divine light of God. Pray for yourself, your family, your community, other people, and also for towns, cities, and countries all around the world.

When prayers are sent with a sincere open heart, divine love will enter and healing will begin to take root where it is most needed. This can be within a person, within a culture, or within a place, so that a positive heal-ing shift eventually begins to take hold. No matter how slow this process may be, *due to the divine laws of evolution and other spiritual factors that interplay,* it is still a favorable move toward the divine light of God. Prayer is the grace we receive for our world and it is the divine will of God to help us without taking away any of our free will power, so that we may consciously choose for ourselves the path of divine light.

There are legions, upon legions, upon legions of God's holy angels who deliver the divine light to our world. They all work under the majestic guidance of the seven magnificent Archangels who preside over the seven divine light frequencies of God. These legions of holy angels will also perform greater celestial acts of divine intervention when instructed by God. Jesus Christ stated: "Do you think I cannot call on my Father, and he will at once put at my disposal more than twelve legions of angels?" (NIV).

Angels do not want to be worshiped or made into any idols; they exist purely to do God's will and they want to help us to align with God's will and His divine plan. Any praise or thanks for the blessings of the angelic power in your life must always be directed to God first. You can also thank the angels for their divine service, just as you would thank your own friends when they help you or give you a blessing. They are holy celestial beings and they deserve our respect. The main point to remember is that it is God who provides you with the angels' blessings.

The Magnificent Celestial Hierarchy

The heaven realms are so vast and because of this any attempt to even simplify the various orders of the holy angels would take so much more detailed information than I can include here. The following exploration of the celestial hierarchy will therefore focus on two very important species and orders of angels that are especially concerned with humanity and with helping us to heal: the majestic Archangels and the extraordinary guardian angels.

The Guardian Angels

For He shall give His angels charge over you, to keep you in all your ways.

—Psalm: 91:11 (NKJV)

The word *angel* is derived from the Greek word *angelos,* meaning messenger. Guardian angels have a very beautiful energy frequency that exudes divine love and a special kind of radiance due to their own unique character and their present depth of divine knowledge, wisdom, and understanding. This spiritual radiance can be perceived as a glowing light emanating from deep within their ethereal bodies and containing different colored rainbow hues, of which there will also be an overall dominant color frequency. This dominant color frequency is geared toward their individual nature and celestial personalities. They were not all created to be alike; otherwise they would have no distinction among them. Angels are just as alive as we are, albeit in a celestial and ethereal sense. They are not robotically designed and they do not belong to the make believe world of fairy tales.

You have one prominent guardian angel who is sent to you by God to help guard, guide, and protect you throughout your life's journey. Many other angels will come to help you depending on the prayers you send and on your specific needs and requirements. Your chief guardian angel will always be in control of any other divine assistance you receive, as you are their personal charge. They love you unconditionally, they know your soul better than anyone else does, and they will never leave you. We can think of our guardian angels as our most dear and sincere best friends. They are responsible for all communication between us and the divine spiritual hierarchy, and they are known as holy messengers or divine messengers.

The guardian angels also receive important divine instruction and guidance directly from the higher ranked Archangels concerning us. Part of your official guardian angel's divine task is to help you become more conscious of your own spiritual connection to a higher power, so you can remember *who you are* as a human soul. It is completely impossible for us *not* to be connected to God, because we are always connected to God. However, it is totally possible for us to be out of alignment with a higher power due to our forgetfulness.

We also easily move out of alignment with a higher power and therefore out of spiritual balance, whenever our thoughts, words, beliefs, habits, behaviors, emotions and actions do not agree with divine truth and divine love. The guardian angels will do their best to help us awaken spiritually without interfering in our free will. They will also attempt to divinely influence us to move back in alignment whenever we seem to be going off track. This is the divine assistance that God gave us to help lovingly steer us throughout our lives. By awakening to who we are, we will become more conscious of our own participation within the divine plan of God. We can then begin to make great strides forward in our spiritual evolution.

Guardian Angels Deliver Divine Guidance

Our guardian angel will attempt to reach our waking consciousness by delivering divine guidance directly to our soul. Our soul will in turn attempt to influence our body and mind with this divine guidance. The difficulty with this is that we need to be self-aware enough to pay attention. Our ego and personality can also override any divine guidance we receive because we have the free will to choose differently. Divine guidance will always be in alignment with God's divine laws—and therefore it will always be for our greatest good. Here is how the actual process plays out.

Our guardian angel will transfer divine frequencies directly to our soul. At this spiritual level divine frequencies are transmitted as *energy and light,* which carry the specialized information and guidance being delivered. Our soul and body are intimately connected and inter-related as they both require each other to experience a physical life existence. (We have a fascinating spiritual and energetic anatomy, which you will discover all about in the next chapter.) Our soul will then begin to process these celestial frequencies at a subtle spiritual and energetic level. Once processed, our soul will transmit this specialized information to our body by merging with the brain and nervous system.

Both hemispheres of the brain—*our rational mind and creative mind*—will instantly begin to register these divine impressions. They will then become automatically adjusted into positive thoughts, inspirational ideas, new perceptions and concepts, and intuitive feelings—the language we all understand. This entire spiritual process enables our guardian angel to help influence our waking consciousness. Oftentimes, what we believe to be our own bright ideas is in fact the divine influence of our guardian angel helping to inspire us.

Why Do Bad Things Happen to Good People if They Have Guardian Angels?

The guardian angels are probably most famously known for their spiritual role in divinely protecting us. I am often asked the following question: If we have guardian angels sent to protect us from harm and accidental death or murder, then where are these guardian angels when bad things happen to good people? Millions of people contemplate and struggle with this question during their lifetime. In my early 20s, I continuously prayed about this question, but I never got an answer that I was totally satisfied with. I was always left with a strong impression and intuitive feeling that I was unable to receive such knowledge at my current level of spiritual understanding. I continued to evolve my soul, and it was years later before I finally received some divine insight into this matter.

It was during my meditation while contemplating this difficult question yet again that I immediately sensed a powerful shift of energy taking place in the atmosphere around me. I knew I was in the presence of an Archangel. My mind was quickly impressed with the following information that arrived as a steady stream of consistent, fast-flowing thoughts. These thoughts were also accompanied by an overwhelming feeling of divine peace and love. I then wrote down the essence of what I received in the following divine message.

A Divine Angelic Message

There are many spiritual factors, forces and divine laws at play that you are unable to comprehend from your limited human perspective. Some of these reasons do prevent us angels from having the power to intervene in such matters. In the event of a person's traumatic death or murder, their guardian angel will immediately guide their soul safely onward to the heaven realms. Only then can a deeper understanding of their death be revealed to them as they awaken to remember who they truly are. For those loved ones who are grieving, spiritually broken, and angry at their loss, they will also be surrounded by many angels who will shower them in the divine light of God.

This divine power will assist them in moving through their trauma and in healing their deep emotional pain. God is always in control and when you are able to let go of the need to deeply understand such matters, then you will discover a greater level of faith and peace. God's love can be clearly witnessed in the powerful actions of people who are so affected by their tragic loss that they go on to become a beacon of light and strength for others who find themselves afflicted in a similar situation. The guardian angels will always intervene whenever they can in agreement with the spiritual factors, forces and divine laws that interplay. The divine blessing is that many times people are often saved from harm without them ever knowing.

As fast as the thoughts came, they just as quickly ended. The message also made me think about several instances in my own life when I was personally saved from harm, including from what could have been a near-fatal car crash. I felt deep gratitude for my guardian angel. Our guardian angels really do work behind the scenes of our life to help us without us ever knowing. How many times have you or your loved ones personally encountered any close calls? If so, this was probably the time when your guardian angel intervened to help prevent what could have been a dire or fatal outcome. People who have been badly injured, often remark they must have had a guardian angel watching over them who saved them from their impending death.

Others swear that an angelic presence intervened and saved their life when they heard a commanding voice delivering specific instructions for them to quickly move, wake up, turn around, stop, and so forth. Our guardian angels are always with us through any illness we experience, any trauma and shock we encounter, and any operations we have. In my 20s, I clearly remember an angelic presence moving around my hospital bed during my recuperation. I saw a very quick physical glimpse of a beautiful female angel checking in on me and helping me to heal. At first I thought she was a nurse, until of course my conscious glimpse of her quickly disappeared before my very eyes. I knew in my heart and soul it was my guardian angel.

Eben Alexander, a neurosurgeon and the *New York Times*–bestselling author of the smash hit book *Proof of Heaven*, had an extremely close call when he was parachuting with a skydiving team in his college years. Eben had less than a fraction of a second to react when another parachutist, who was unaware that Eben was up above him, opened their main chute and headed straight toward him. A collision seemed inevitable due to the speed and force of them both moving through the air so quickly. This would have been disastrous and could have easily resulted in death or severe injury for both men, had Eben not reacted so imminently. Eben believes it was a much deeper part of him that saved his life that day, other than his brain reacting to an emergency situation, when he somehow managed to move out of the way with time to spare. He felt that time slowed down and that his mind watched the action as if he was watching a movie play in slow motion.

I have personally experienced this slow-motion response during a near-fatal car crash, so I could instantly recognize this exact same scenario. Our guardian angel will always work directly with our soul to save us in an emergency that we are not destined to experience. It was divinely written for you to receive this celestial protection before you were even born.

Aligning With Your Guardian Angel

Angels are God's messengers who intercede with God on our behalf. When we align with our guardian angel we automatically go direct to God. And, when we go direct to God, we will automatically align with our guardian angel, even when we are unaware of this process. Our love and devotion for God will help to strengthen the spiritual bond held between us and our angel. Guardian angels help us to align with the divine power so we may bridge the gap in consciousness between us and God. All prayers to God are witnessed by the angels, and all sincere prayers are answered by God and involve the celestial support of the angels. By consciously aligning with the divine energy frequency of our guardian angel, we can begin to actively "charge up" the spiritual power of our soul with more of God's divine light frequencies.

We can use these divine light frequencies to help us address our health complaints and life issues. You can think of this as your participation in the co-creation of improving the state of your health and your life. So aligning with your guardian angel is all about your ability to consciously co-create with a higher power—a divine power. You can talk to your guardian angel in an informal, friendly manner and ask them to help you with any issues you are presently struggling with. As previously mentioned, they are your best spiritual friends.

The following divine exercise will include a more formal approach of using divine prayer decrees to begin your initial alignment with your guardian angel. Divine Prayer decrees are used as a very powerful procedure for activating divine law. Its underlying principle carries the divine message of *"ask with spiritual authority and faith and it will be given unto you."* This divine process will especially help you to draw through God's divine light to assist you in all your ways. You can say the prayers silently and at any time, and all that is required from you is a sincere open heart. It really is that simple. However, it is more powerful when you speak the prayers aloud.

When your energy is in a relaxed and harmonious state your consciousness has more spiritual power to align with the divine inspiration of your guardian angel. Use the following very easy energetic technique to help prepare your consciousness before you say the divine prayer decrees.

Angel Medicine Energy Relaxation and Balancing Technique

Use this energetic technique to help you:

» Center and harmonize the energies of your mind, body, and soul.

» Empower your self-expression.

Time: approximately 2 minutes

» Begin with your hands held in prayer position over the center of your chest and heart area. Take several deep breaths, breathing in through your nose and out of your mouth to help relax your body and mind. This energetic process will instantly help to center and balance your energies (heart and soul).

» After one minute, move your hands, *keeping them in prayer position,* to the center of your throat, with your index fingers in alignment with and near to your bottom lip (not touching). Again take a few deep breaths and relax.

» This action will assist in energizing the power of your spoken words due to your hand position being centered within a powerful energy vortex located in the throat, and associated with your self-expression. This energy center in its most developed expression is also associated with divine will. It can help you to align your will with the will of God. Stay like this for one minute and while you say the following divine prayer decrees.

Guardian Angel Divine Alignment Decree

Use this divine exercise to help you:

» Align your consciousness with your guardian angel.

» Receive divine inspiration.

Time: approximately 20 seconds

"Guardian angel of mine, I choose to align my mind, heart and soul with your divine inspiration. I decree that this be in agreement with the will of God, and for my greatest good. Amen! It is done. It is done. It is done. (Thank you, God. Thank you, guardian angel.)"

Guardian Angel Divine Healing Decree

Use this divine exercise to help you:

» Activate divine healing power.

» Receive divine inspiration.

Time: approximately 20 seconds

"Guardian angel of mine, I ask that my soul receive divine healing frequencies to help me in all my ways. I decree that this be in agreement with the will of God, and for my greatest good. Amen! It is done. It is done. It is done. (Thank you, God. Thank you, guardian angel.)"

You have just set in motion the conscious activation to receive divine healing frequencies. These powerful healing frequencies will be condensed in measure in accordance with the soul's requirement. You can say the guardian angel divine healing decree before you go to sleep each night and you will receive the rejuvenating divine healing frequencies when your body is relaxed and at rest, making it extra beneficial. Your soul can make use of this extra power to serve you in all your ways, as previously petitioned.

The angelic role of them transferring divine healing frequencies is what enables God's power to go to work immediately within all areas of your health and your life. This divine help will be administered at first on a more subtle spiritual and energetic level, constantly working behind the scenes of your life until it becomes a firm part of your physical reality. It is the beginning of you forging a more conscious and powerful connection to your soul, your guardian angel, the divine powers of heaven, and almighty God.

Now that you have consciously aligned with your guardian angel you can also ask that they give you a clear tangible sign of their divine service. This request is less formal:

"Guardian angel of mine. Please give me a clear sign that you have received my divine prayer decree!"

Evidential Angelic Sign

You will most likely receive the sign of a white feather, either the same day or within a few days of asking. The white feather is the most universally accepted angel sign because most people tend to picture angels as celestial looking humans with white feathered wings. This is due to the renaissance art period in which beautiful paintings of angelic beings were created with wings and with halos of light surrounding their heads. Some angels do have wings, as mentioned in the Bible with the seraphim: *"Above him were seraphim, each with six wings: With two wings they covered their faces, with two they covered their feet, and with two they were flying." (Isaiah 6:2 (NIV))*. Angels do *not* need any wings to fly and move about, and what we have come to interpret as white, feathered wings are simply beautiful streams of divine light emanating from their celestial bodies.

However, the angels also know that we have come to associate them with their exquisite feathered wings, and so they are very happy to appear to us in this way to help us feel more comfortable with our perceptions. They are neither male nor female, although they will joyfully take on the appearance of a man or woman if necessary. In this case they will radiate their beauty as a perfect-looking human, with or without wings. Other evidential signs to know that the angels have received your request and are answering you can include:

» Seeing butterflies, dragonflies, and robins close by.

» Witnessing angel images appearing in the formation of clouds.

» Seeing a statue or an ornament of an angel.

» Hearing a song about angels.

» Seeing a film about angels.

» Receiving an angel gift of some kind, such as a painting, a book, or an item of jewelry.

Any angelic sign that you receive will also be accompanied by a divine knowing that the sign is especially for you backed up by a wonderful, positive, and supportive feeling. In my previous book, *The Power of Angels,* I have an entire chapter dedicated to the subject of angel signs.

Your guardian angel is the most joyful, enthusiastic, and jubilant celestial being, and they are just elated to divinely assist you. They will do whatever they can for you while also keeping in agreement with God's divine laws and with your soul's evolutionary path. They truly are a divine gift and blessing from God.

Now that you have been introduced to your very own guardian angel, it is time to discover all about the astonishing celestial power of the magnificent and divinely inspirational Archangels. Whereas the guardian angels can be thought of us our angelic best friends, the

Archangels can be thought of as brilliant divine teachers, extremely powerful healing experts, and the stunning celestial embodiment of God's creative power.

The Mighty Archangels

The Archangels are astonishingly magnificent in their divine design. They have a rarefied and breathtaking beauty and human-like appearance in face and body. They are much taller than the guardian angels, who in turn are also taller than we humans. The Archangels are extremely powerful because they have been awarded great spiritual authority by God to perform important heavenly duties. The divine light emanating from their celestial bodies shines brightly with their divine love, spiritual power, knowledge, and wisdom. This is what gives the Archangels their majestic and mighty presence. There are countless Archangels existing within the celestial hierarchy, but for the purpose of this divine healing book, I will include the seven exalted Archangels who preside over the seven unique frequencies of God's divine light.

God's Seven Frequencies of Divine Light

The divine light of God is the most exquisite, sublime, dynamic, spectacular, and potent power that exists bar none. Not even the ultraviolet light streams that blaze from the rays of the sun come even marginally close. God's glorious divine light is divided into seven potent frequencies that are direct emanations of God's divine power. Each individual stream of divine light contains one of seven different aspects and attributes of God's almighty consciousness. This is how tremendously powerful, immense, and divinely awesome this light truly is in helping us to heal and repair our health and our lives. It is the most powerful medicine we can ever hope to receive—a divine medicine.

God has assigned seven of His notable Archangels to be the celestial embodiment of each individual stream of divine light. The divine light of God in its glory and magnificence is whole. Before it enters the atmosphere of the earth it is filtered into seven specialized colored frequencies similar to the colors you observe in the beauty of a rainbow, but much more splendid. Each specialized frequency of divine light contains extraordinary transformational and miraculous healing power, which each Archangel can transmit directly to our soul. The powerful influence of the light can then help us to increase our own innate spiritual power to activate divine healing. All seven divine healing frequencies can truly help us in the most outstanding, superb, and diverse ways.

Divine Energy Download

We receive these specialized frequencies of divine light in the exact same way as previously described with the guardian angels. The only difference is that they are more potent and powerful in every single way. We can think of this celestial process as a divine energy download that upgrades all of our systems—our spiritual, energetic, and physical anatomies. We are a dazzling mixture of spiritual, mental, emotional, and physical energies, which you will explore more fully in the next chapter. Through consciously aligning with the seven superior Archangels, we can receive expert healing guidance and spectacular healing power.

The Seven Archangels and Their Divine Light Frequencies

Archangel Michael

Archangel Michael is the greatest and most revered of the angels, and is probably the best known Archangel of all. His name means "he who is like God." He is a mighty angelic leader in charge of all the Archangels, guardian angels, and other celestial beings. He is known as Prince, Captain, or Chief of the angels. His energy is abundantly strong, immensely powerful, and divinely protective. His divine power can help us to align our will with the will of God. Archangel Michael is placed in celestial charge of the first frequency of divine light. This powerful frequency manifests as a brilliant royal blue light, which emanates from deep within his glorious celestial body. The first frequency is the grand embodiment of divine truth and God's almighty power. Here are several examples of what this dynamic frequency of divine light can personally help you with, followed by a specific divine prayer decree to immediately activate divine healing.

Physical Healing

» Viruses and any other destructive influences that invade and attack the body.

» Endocrine system problems.

» Chronic pain and inflammation.

» High blood pressure.

Psychological Healing

» Addictions of all kinds, and any destructive habits and behaviors that are toxic to your soul.

» To help you overcome all limiting beliefs that are out of alignment with divine truth.

» To help you develop courage and confidence to live your truth.

» To help diminish any fear, anger, and hatred.

Spiritual Healing

» Spiritual and energetic protection.

» Depression.

» Karmic healing for health and life issues that continuously persist (more about this in Chapter 5).

Personal Blessings

» Divine protection (physical and spiritual).

» Develop leadership qualities.

» To help you align your will with the will of God so that you can co-create your life in agreement with a higher power and discover your life purpose. (Your life will then flow with more ease.)

» Deepen your faith in God.

Divine Prayer Decree to Align With Archangel Michael

"Archangel Michael, I ask that my soul receive the royal blue divine light frequency to help me heal in all my ways for my greatest and highest good. (You can also be specific with what you need help with.) *I decree that this is in agreement with the will of God. Amen! It is done. It is done. It is done."* (Thank you, God. Thank you, Archangel Michael.)

Finish by quickly visualizing (a few seconds) your entire body, inside and out, being bathed in a royal blue light.

Archangel Jophiel

Archangel Jophiel's name translates as "beauty of God." He is an extremely wise and enlightened Archangel who can help us to align our mind with the mind of God. Archangel Jophiel is placed in celestial charge of the second frequency of divine light. This powerful frequency manifests as a brilliant golden yellow light, which emanates from deep within his glorious celestial body. The second frequency is the remarkable embodiment of divine wisdom and God's inspiration. Here are some examples of what this powerful frequency of divine light can personally help you with, followed by a specific divine prayer decree to immediately activate divine healing.

Physical Healing

» Brain problems.

» Nervous system disorders.

» Skeletal problems.

» Headaches; migraines.

» Insomnia and sleep disorders.

» Skin complaints.

» Fibromyalgia.

Psychological Healing

» Limiting and false beliefs.

» Schizophrenia.

» Anxiety disorders.

» Phobias and panic disorders.

» Post-traumatic stress.

Spiritual Healing

» Depression.

Personal Blessings

» To help you align with your higher self.

» To illuminate and inspire your mind with beautiful ideas.

» To enlighten your soul with divine knowledge and wisdom.

» To help you perceive yourself, your life, others, and the world in a more positive light.

» To help you study, understand, and retain knowledge.

Divine Prayer Decree to Align With Archangel Jophiel

"Archangel Jophiel, I ask that my soul receive the golden yellow divine light frequency to help me heal in all my ways for my greatest and highest good. (You can also be specific with what you need help with.) *I decree that this is in agreement with the will of God. Amen! It is done. It is done. It is done."* *(Thank you, God. Thank you, Archangel Jophiel.)*

Finish by quickly visualizing (a few seconds) your entire body, inside and out, being bathed in golden yellow light.

Archangel Chamuel

Archangel Chamuel's name translates as "he who sees God." This beautiful Archangel is placed in celestial charge of the third frequency of divine light. This powerful frequency manifests as a beautiful rose pink light, which emanates from deep within his glorious celestial body. The third frequency is the stunning embodiment of divine love and God's mercy and compassion. Here are some examples of what this powerful frequency of divine light can personally help you with, followed by a specific divine prayer decree to immediately activate divine healing.

Physical Healing

» All illness and disease.

» Heart problems.

» Circulation issues.

» Blood problems; blood count issues.

» Lung issues.

» Immune system issues.

» Cancer (specifically breast cancer and lung cancer).

Psychological Healing

» Heal the emotional pain of heartache and grief through loss.

» Heal a broken heart due to relationship breakups, separation, or divorce.

» Heal the emotional issues concerned with self-hatred.

» Heal painful memories.

Spiritual Healing

» Depression.

» Forgiveness issues.

Personal Blessings

>> Find true love.

>> Repair and deepen the love you already have.

>> Mend and heal family rifts and arguments; settle disputes.

>> To help you end a relationship amicably.

>> Open up your energy to divine love, compassion, and radiant joy.

Divine Prayer Decree to Align With Archangel Chamuel

"Archangel Chamuel, I ask that my soul receive the rose pink divine light frequency to help me heal in all my ways for my greatest and highest good. (You can also be specific with what you need help with.) *I decree that this is in agreement with the will of God. Amen! It is done. It is done. It is done."* (Thank you, God. Thank you, Archangel Chamuel.)

Finish by quickly visualizing (a few seconds) your entire body, inside and out, being bathed in rose pink light.

Archangel Gabriel

Archangel Gabriel's name translates as "God is my strength." This wonderful Archangel is placed in celestial charge of the fourth frequency of divine light. This powerful frequency manifests as a pure white light, which emanates from deep within his glorious celestial body. The fourth frequency is the splendid embodiment of divine purity and God's perfection. Here are some examples of what this powerful frequency of divine light can personally help you with, followed by a specific divine prayer decree to immediately activate divine healing.

Physical Healing

» All illness and disease.

» Assist you with a physical detox to clear all toxins from the body.

» Issues regarding infertility.

» Kidney problems.

Psychological Healing

» Purify ungodly thoughts and feelings.

» Purify your fears.

Spiritual Healing

» Depression.

Personal Blessings

» Strength, hope, and any encouragement you need.

» To be more disciplined.

» To be more joyful.

Divine Prayer Decree to Align With Archangel Gabriel

"Archangel Gabriel, I ask that my soul receive the pure white divine light frequency to help me heal in all my ways for

my greatest and highest good. (You can also be specific with what you need help with.) *I decree that this is in agreement with the will of God. Amen! It is done. It is done. It is done."* *(Thank you, God. Thank you, Archangel Gabriel.)*

Finish by quickly visualizing (a few seconds) your entire body, inside and out, being bathed in pure white light.

Archangel Raphael

Archangel Raphael's name translates as "God heals." This amazing divine healing Archangel is placed in celestial charge of the fifth frequency of divine light. This powerful frequency manifests as a brilliant emerald green light, which emanates from deep within his glorious celestial body. The fifth frequency is the miraculous embodiment of God's divine healing medicine. Here are some examples of what this powerful frequency of divine light can personally help you with, followed by a specific divine prayer decree to immediately activate divine healing.

Physical Healing

- » All illness and disease.
- » Brain problems.
- » Nervous system issues.
- » Eye issues.
- » Ear issues.
- » Insomnia.

Psychological Healing

- » Releasing your irrational fears.

- » Clearing your false perceptions.

- » Healing painful memories.

- » Balancing both hemispheres of the brain.

Spiritual Healing

- » Depression.

Personal Blessings

- » Divine protection during your travels.

- » Increase abundance in your life.

- » Open up your energy to divine insight.

Divine Prayer Decree to Align With Archangel Raphael

"Archangel Raphael, I ask that my soul receive the emerald green divine light frequency to help me heal in all my ways for my greatest and highest good. (You can also be specific with what you need help with.) *I decree that this is in agreement with the will of God. Amen! It is done. It is done. It is done."* (Thank you, God. Thank you, Archangel Raphael.)

Finish by quickly visualizing (a few seconds) your entire body, inside and out, being bathed in emerald green light.

Note: Always ask Archangel Raphael to help oversee and intervene in the healing work of any doctors, medical professionals, dentists, and healers that you have appointments with.

Archangel Uriel

Archangel Uriel's name translates as "fire or light of God." This peaceful and extraordinary Archangel is placed in celestial charge of the sixth frequency of divine light. This powerful frequency manifests as a vibrant purple-gold-ruby light, which emanates from deep within his glorious celestial body. The sixth frequency of divine light is the glorious embodiment of divine peace and service. Here are some examples of what this powerful frequency of divine light can personally help you with, followed by a specific divine prayer decree to immediately activate divine healing.

Physical Healing

» Stomach problems.

» Liver problems.

» Gall bladder problems.

» Nervous system issues.

Psychological Healing

» Freedom from self-condemnation.

» Freedom from personal struggles (destructive self-indulging habits/behaviors).

» Freedom from the need to control.

» Freedom from fear.

» Transform your inability to establish peaceful, harmonious relationships.

Spiritual Healing

» Depression.

Personal Blessings

» Divine service (helping you to serve God and others).

» Open up your energy to inner peace.

Divine Prayer Decree to Align With Archangel Uriel

"Archangel Uriel, I ask that my soul receive the purple-gold-ruby divine light frequency to help me heal in all my ways for my greatest and highest good. (You can also be specific with what you need help with.) *I decree that this is in agreement with the will of God. Amen! It is done. It is done. It is done."* (Thank you, God. Thank you, Archangel Uriel.)

Finish by quickly visualizing (a few seconds) your entire body, inside and out, being bathed in purple and gold light.

Archangel Zadkiel

Archangel Zadkiel's name translates as "righteousness of God." This benevolent and powerful Archangel is placed in celestial charge of the seventh frequency of divine light. This divine frequency manifests as a tremendously powerful violet light, which emanates from deep within his glorious celestial body. The seventh frequency of divine light is the sensational embodiment of divine mercy, freedom, forgiveness, and God's transformational power. Here are some examples of what this powerful frequency of divine light can personally help you with, followed by a specific divine prayer decree to immediately activate divine healing.

Physical Healing

» Terminal illness.

» All illness and disease.

» Reproductive system issues.

» Chronic pain.

» Transmute the chemical side effects of prescription drugs.

» Food poisoning.

» Transmute and purify all toxins in the body.

Psychological Healing

» Transmute discordant negative thoughts.

» Clear resentments.

» Clear painful memories.

» Transform false beliefs.

» Transform destructive behavioral patterns and habits.

» Freedom from guilt.

» Freedom from addictions of all kinds.

Spiritual Healing

» Forgiveness issues.

» Transformation.

» Open up your energy to radiant joy.

» Karmic healing for health and life issues that continuously persist (more about this in Chapter 5).

Personal Blessings

» To receive God's grace and mercy.

» God's justice.

Divine Prayer Decree to Align With Archangel Zadkiel

"Archangel Zadkiel, I ask that my soul receive the violet divine light frequency to help me heal in all my ways for my greatest and highest good. (You can also be specific with what you need help with.) *I decree that this is in agreement with the will of God. Amen! It is done. It is done. It is done."* *(Thank you, God. Thank you, Archangel Zadkiel.)*

Finish by quickly (a few seconds) visualizing your entire body, inside and out, being bathed in violet light.

By regularly using these magnificent divine prayer decrees each day you will seriously help to increase the divine light of God within your consciousness to help you heal. Never underestimate the potent power within the divine light of God to personally help you in all your ways.

❧

From exploring just a small part of the magnificent celestial hierarchy you can easily see and begin to comprehend the amazing spiritual assistance and divine healing power that is freely made available to us. God's holy angels are more than happy to help us, as in doing so they also help us to evolve our human souls in accordance with the divine plan. Now that you have been introduced to the angels, it is time to explore the complex and dazzling structure of our fascinating spiritual and energetic anatomy. In Chapter 2 you will discover a whole new range of energy skills to help get your energies moving, buzzing, and more vitalized.

Chapter Two

Our Divine Design

You don't have a soul. You are a Soul. You have a body.

—C.S. Lewis

We as human beings are God's masterpiece and work of art. The blueprint for our physical body is created by divine mind—the great architect of all creation. God's intelligence and love have created the perfect human form through a process of divine design, which includes divine light to pattern our physical bodies, cosmic substance to build our physical bodies, and God's life force to maintain and sustain our physical bodies. In this chapter you will come to discover all about your own amazing spiritual and energetic anatomy to help you become more familiarized with your energies. You will then be able to actively work with these divine forces and the energies of creation that are already within you, to help you establish a greater level of energetic resonance and harmony.

When all of your energies and subtle forces are running smoothly, free from any restrictions, and are flowing in divine harmony together, then you will instantly increase your level of vitality. You need a healthy level of vitality to enable your body to establish enough energetic power for it to heal and repair itself. With this increase in vitality you will automatically and naturally improve any existing health issues you currently have, and you will effortlessly help to prevent any further complaints from developing. Looking after your own energies is therefore enormously beneficial, and is a wonderful, safe, and nontoxic form of preventive medicine. You will soon discover several simple and powerful divine healing exercises and energetic techniques to help get your energies moving. This is all very exciting for you if you have never worked on adjusting your own energies before.

Our Divine Makeup

The Word, Voice, and Sound of God created the heavens and the earth, and all the host of them. God said, "Let there be light," and from separating day and night, He continued to make the entire structure and form of the earth and all of its inhabitants, including us. Our physical body and form—every atom, molecule, particle, and cellular structure—are the enlightened, created results of divine intelligence, cosmic substance, and the breath of God. *"And the LORD God formed man of the dust of the* ground, and breathed into his nostrils the breath of life; and man became a living soul." (Genesis: 2:7 (KJB))*. The dust from the ground is symbolic of the cosmic material and substance of the universal energies of creation used to create the human form. God also created us in His own image. *"So God created mankind in His own image, in the image of God He created them; male and female He created them." (Genesis: 1:27 (NIV))*.

Therefore we are an individual portion of divine design and a divine particle of God. We are a living breathing soul infused with the divine essence and spirit of God encased in a physical body so we may have a physical life experience. We are created from divine mind with divine love, we did not create ourselves. We are powerful beyond measure and we have unlimited infinite possibilities for growth.

God created, patterned, and molded everything by divine design according to its own kind. Everything that exists within the universe is always in a continuing state of evolution, and the universe is able to keep expanding and growing as a result of this. The big debate over creation verses evolution continues. God is the Creator and He did create everything in this universe, *including* the process of evolution and the divine laws governing over evolution. People who seriously debate this subject will only look to the one side that is in alignment with their beliefs, while completely dismissing or researching the other. The not-so-difficult secret is that God is in both. This is God's universe and this is God's evolution. Let me repeat that one more time: God is in both!

Our Divinely Created Physical Body

The divine pattern of our created physical body is exactly the same design for every single one of us because that is what makes us a human soul in comparison to that of an animal, a rock, a star, or a planet. Our original divine patterning as a physical body is always perfect, as God intended and created our bodies to be healthy and whole. Today's hereditary factors and weaknesses in our physiology stem from energetic malfunctions to our original body's blueprint, which has already happened somewhere along our ancestry line and is passed through the evolutionary process of our human DNA.

Our body's DNA determines our current predetermined level of physical health and vitality. It is what helps to shape the etheric cellular structure and nervous system, and form of our physical body during conception. God always holds the original divine template and perfect vision for our physical body and health in divine mind empowered by divine love. This is absolutely fantastic news for us because when we work with the energies of creation, we can help to correct and adjust any interference in our body's energy patterns by aligning our consciousness with our original divine blueprint. It is God's will for your body to be healthy and whole, as it was originally designed to be.

Our Divinely Created Soul (Spiritual DNA)

We have both spiritual DNA and human DNA that directly impact our health. Other factors that typically affect our health include our environment and the actions of our own free will (unbalanced nutrition, destructive lifestyle habits, and so on). Our soul contains our spiritual DNA, which determines our current level of consciousness that has continuously evolved from the very moment in which we because individualized souls created by God. We are not born blank slates; we have existed before this life and we will continue to exist after this life.

Within our spiritual DNA we store all of our previous experiences, memories, the lessons we have learned along the way, our karmic patterns, and what we still need to overcome, correct, and address within our soul to help us evolve. Our spiritual DNA directly influences our physical body after conception by providing subtle energetic patterns that are written into our brain, nervous system, and etheric design. These spiritual patterns govern over our body's health as well as governing over our life's theme. Our life's theme can be considered to be our specific life purpose, which covers our soul's intentions for this particular life time.

The spiritual merging of our soul to our body via our brain, nervous system, and heart enables our body and mind to become alive with our consciousness. Without our soul our body could not survive, and without our body our soul could not gain a physical experience. Both kinds of DNA (physical and spiritual) therefore directly influence and are both responsible for our divine design during and after conception—our *mind, body, and spirit.* And both will determine the cellular structure and vitality of our physical form. From this you can easily see that we have both a physical and a spiritual energetic anatomy. Our body's state of health and well-being therefore directly contends with both our physical and our spiritual stages of evolution (blood line and soul line). The majority of the medical profession will only tend to address our physical anatomy, completely dismissing the energetic design and spiritual nature of our soul.

Our Divine Heritage

Within our spiritual DNA, we always contain our pure divine heritage—*our divine spark of God.* We can activate this divine power within us through aligning our consciousness with divine truth and divine love. Our spiritual DNA will then begin to animate every cell of our physical body with God's divine force. Health issues can be easily restored and healing miracles can and do happen with regard to overcoming genetic challenges, disorders, illness, and disease. Anything is entirely possible through the divine healing power of God. You will discover more about your spiritual DNA in Chapter 5, in which we will explore the deeper patterns of healing with the superbly powerful angel healing experts.

Our Spiritual and Energetic Anatomy

As body and soul, we are an intricate and complex mixture of cosmic frequencies and forces made up of subtle energy fields, subtle energy bodies, electromagnetic frequencies, energetic systems, and energy pathways. All of these combined energies need to work, flow, and blend together in balanced harmony to help maintain the divine patterning, integrity, and vitality of the physical body's structure and form. Whenever there is an energetic disturbance in any singular part of our spiritual and energetic anatomy, it will alter the flow and affect the whole. We will then begin to feel off balance and out of sync with the natural rhythm of our health and our life. Angel medicine exercises and energetic techniques are especially formulated to help bring balance back to an out-of-sync, overly taxed, spiritually depleted, and energetically stressed bodily rhythm. Let's take a closer look at our incredible and entangled energies.

Our Energy Systems, Our Energy Pathways, and Our Subtle Energy Bodies

Our body's subtle anatomy is profoundly and divinely intelligent.

We are divinely fashioned by God's creative power. Our spiritual and energetic anatomy is a multifaceted complex work of divine art, of which all systems depend on each other for us to function at an optimum vibrational frequency. This overall vibrational frequency is the sum total of our consciousness (mind, body, and soul). We totally thrive on a physical level when our vibrational frequency is vibrant, and all of our systems are running, processing, flowing, pulsating, connecting, and crossing over in beautiful harmony with one another. Our energies are divinely intelligent and they know exactly what to do to help us heal when they are all in happy sync with one another. Problems arise with our health and well-being when our energies become energetically stressed and vulnerable, shifting us out of rhythm.

The following is a very basic look at what makes up our entire spiritual and energetic anatomy, along with some easy-to-use divine exercises and energetic techniques to help you get started with your healing. It is not necessary for you to completely and deeply understand all about your spiritual and energetic anatomy for these exercises to work, as they will still certainly work. It does, however, help to familiarize you with your divinely created and awe-inspired energies. Our amazing spiritual and energetic anatomy can be broken down as follows:

» **The etheric energy body:** the energetic power that is the matrix for our cellular growth.

» **The body's seven main energy centers:** energetic stations that hold light and energy.

» **The body's energetic pathways:** a network of subtle channels that carry light and energy.

» **Subtle energy bodies and energy fields:** our soul and our spiritual, mental, and emotional states. Known in its entirety as our bio-auric field.

» **Our higher-self:** the highest part of our spiritual nature and Christ consciousness.

Our Etheric Energy Body
(We can help our cells.)

We each have an etheric energy body, which is the divine patterning held in place for the shape, structure, and function of our physical form. It is the foundation for all of our energy systems, and is what directly influences the health and life of our body. Our physical body would not exist without this etheric patterning in place because it serves as the energetic matrix for our cellular growth—from which our body's tissues and organs are shaped and formed. In this case, we can perceive that the physical body is the end result of the etheric form and is not prior to the etheric form. It looks like a blueprint for an architect's design as its appearance is formed of many different lines of bluish light that crisscross and network together to form an intricate energy grid.

When the energetic condition of the etheric body is compromised it will automatically affect all other energy systems because it is their main foundation. By energetically working with the etheric body, we can help to repair any dysfunctional patterns of energies and restore the vital energy flow. This will be of enormous benefit to all the other energy systems, and will especially help to support the health and integrity of our physical body. You will discover an extremely powerful angel medicine exercise to help repair the etheric energy body in Chapter 5, and the results of this exercise can often be felt instantaneous.

Our Body's Seven Main Energy Centers
(We can help our organs, systems, and body parts.)

We have seven main energy centers that are tremendous energetic power stations for our physical body. These energy centers, when working at optimum frequency, enable God's life force to enter freely into the physical body and to circulate abundantly throughout our other energy systems. As well as our own predetermined supply of vitality derived from our spiritual and physical DNA, God also sends us a steady stream of life force through the elements of nature. With each brand new day there is always a constant abundance of God's life force freely given to us to help sustain us.

Our seven main energy centers are firmly embedded within the etheric energy body, which, as previously mentioned, is the foundation for all other energy systems. They look like spiraling whirlpools and vortexes of light and color. They create their own subtle energy fields as well being associated with one of the seven main subtle energy bodies. The wider part of the energy center extends outward, away from the body. The narrow end of the spiraling vortex reaches deep into the physical body and connects with a central energy channel that runs in alignment with the base of the spine to the top of the head.

They have a direct physiological correspondence to the body through their influence on the major endocrine glands and our nervous system. Therefore, each one of the seven main energy centers governs over specific areas of the body, regulating and distributing valuable life force to all of its organs and bodily systems. Another one of their prime functions is also directly involved with processing our emotional, psychological, and spiritual states of health. All of our memories and experiences are energetically encoded to their allocated energy centers, and when processed they become part of our spiritual and energetic anatomy according to their nature. This is what constitutes our overall level of consciousness and spiritual evolution.

The energy centers are approximately 3 inches in diameter when in a healthy state of balance. When out of balance their size is impaired, their processing speed is impaired, they shift their usual rotational direction, they alter their dominant color, and their frequency typically weakens. They are then unable to fully complete the important energetic tasks required of them, and our organs, body parts, and bodily systems lose some of their invaluable supportive and sustaining energetic power—resulting in physiological changes.

They will also fail to optimally process new, vibrant life force and transmute old, tired life force that we need to release from our bodies. This immediately impacts the rest of our intricate energy systems, and we can become energetically weak and vulnerable. The physical result of this if ignored and left to continue is a clear outcome of bodily fatigue due to a severe lack of vitality. Immune system suppression and the development of further health issues can then ensure because we will lack the energetic power required by our body for us to repair, rejuvenate, and heal.

The Seven Lamps of God

God gave us these seven remarkable spiritual centers so we can receive and hold His divine light to help nourish and sustain our body, mind, and soul. We receive a steady flow of God's divine light each and every day from the Christ consciousness and through the magnificence of our own higher self—the highest spiritual aspect of our soul that is in constant alignment with God. (You will find out more about your higher self shortly.) The seven main energy centers can therefore be thought of as seven lamps of God's light and power for our body and soul.

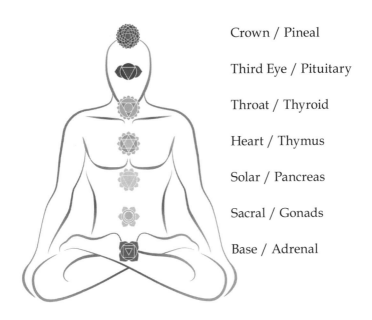

Crown / Pineal

Third Eye / Pituitary

Throat / Thyroid

Heart / Thymus

Solar / Pancreas

Sacral / Gonads

Base / Adrenal

Our seven main energy centers.

Each energy center corresponds to one of God's divine light frequencies and to one of the magnificent Archangels who embodies them. Divine light frequencies have their own glorious colors associated with them, and the energy centers have their own dominant color frequencies. We can use the dominant color associated with each energy center to help us balance their frequency. However, divine light is much more powerful with regard to healing at a deeper core energy level to effect significant changes. Divine light healing work leads to permanent successful changes that help to restructure, repair, and energize each center by providing the necessary divine frequencies and spiritual power to do so.

Archangels and the Energy Centers

The Archangels can transmit a certain portion of God's tremendous divine light to our energy centers. The divine light is so powerful that it can instantly begin to transform unenlightened energies so that they become transmuted and purified. By working with an energy center that directly relates to a specific body part, organ, or system that is suffering, then you can help to send God's divine light and life force right to where they are most needed.

These spiritual energy centers may be a completely new concept to many of you. However, regularly using the Angel Medicine Divine Light Exercise (see page 75) can help to give you some tangible sign of their existence. Within a short period of time, sometimes even days, you will notice a remarked improvement in how you feel, how well you are sleeping, how much more clarity you have, how much more energy you have, and how well your health issues begin to repair and heal. Plus, the divine light will be working on deeper levels as previously mentioned to help bring about permanent results.

Here are the Archangels and their corresponding energy centers, along with a very powerful angel medicine exercise to help you add divine light to each center.

Archangel Jophiel and the Crown Energy Center
- » Located at the top of the head.
- » Physiologically concerned with the pineal gland.
- » Divine light frequency is golden yellow.
- » Divine light works at correcting our false and limiting beliefs.

Archangel Raphael and the Brow Energy Center
- » Located in the center of the forehead.
- » Physiologically concerned with the pituitary gland.
- » Divine light frequency is emerald green.
- » Divine light works at correcting our false perceptions.

Archangel Michael and the Throat Energy Center

» Located in the center of the throat.

» Physiologically concerned with the thyroid gland.

» Divine light frequency is royal blue.

» Divine light works at correcting anything in our self-expression that is out of alignment with divine truth.

Archangel Chamuel and the Heart Energy Center

» Located in the center of the chest.

» Physiologically concerned with the thymus gland.

» Divine light frequency is rose pink.

» Divine light works at correcting anything opposing divine love.

Archangel Uriel and the Solar Plexus Energy Center

» Located just above the navel.

» Physiologically concerned with the pancreas.

» Divine light frequency is purple/gold/ruby.

» Divine light works at correcting our negative thoughts about ourselves, and our indecision and lack of belief and confidence in our own personal power.

Archangel Zadkiel and the Sacral Plexus Energy Center

- » Located just below the navel.

- » Physiologically concerned with the gonads.

- » Divine light frequency is violet.

- » Divine light works at transmuting our repressed and painful emotions.

Archangel Gabriel and the Base Energy Center

- » Located at the base of the spine.

- » Physiologically concerned with the adrenal glands.

- » Divine light frequency is white.

- » Divine light works at correcting and repairing dysfunctional patterns of energy in the etheric subtle body, so energy can be metabolized properly and our physical body vitalized.

Angel Medicine Divine Light Exercise

Use this divine exercise to help you:

- » Free, regulate, and metabolize your energies.

- » Initiate deeper core levels of healing (emotional, psychological, spiritual).

- » Balance your brain chemistry.

» Balance both hemispheres of the brain.

» Calm your nervous system.

» Empower your cells.

» Balance your hormones.

» Empower your immune system.

» Increase your overall vitality.

» Help spiritually repair any physical health issues, illness, and dis-ease.

» Help spiritually heal and ease any aches and pains.

Time: approximately 14 minutes

Start with a divine action and prayer as follows:

Bring your hands together into prayer position with your index fingers in alignment with your bottom lip, but not touching. Say, *"I ask for the white light of the Holy Spirit to surround and protect my body and soul. Thank you God, Amen, or it is done!"*

Now, rub your palms together. Use your right thumb to moderately press the center of your left palm and keep pumping it a few times. (You have a minor energy center in each palm, which will enable you to transmit God's life force and divine light.) Use your left thumb to do the same to your right palm. You have energetically activated both minor centers. Let's begin!

Crown Energy Center Healing

» Gently place both of your palms directly on the crown of your head (side by side), or in a position you find most comfortable. (You cannot do it wrong, as the energy center is located at your crown.)

» State the following divine request: *"I ask Archangel Jophiel to add his divine light to my crown energy center for my greatest and highest good."* Keep your hands in this position for about two minutes. You may begin to feel your palms tingling, getting warmer, and buzzing with energy as God's divine light begins to pour into you. You may feel nothing at all; it doesn't matter, as it will still be working. You are receiving divine healing power and in doing so your energy will never be left the same as it was when you started.

Brow Energy Center Healing

» Next, move your right hand sideways, covering over your forehead, and move your left hand sideways, covering over the lower back of your head near your hair line.

» State the following divine request: *"I ask Archangel Raphael to add his divine light to my brow energy center for my greatest and highest good.*" Keep your hands in this position for about two minutes.

Throat Energy Center Healing

» Next, move your hands so that they both cupped over and facing toward the center of your throat, held about 3 inches away from the body (not touching).

» State the following divine request: *"I ask Archangel Michael to add his divine light to my throat energy center for my greatest and highest good.*" Keep your hands in this position for about two minutes.

Heart Energy Center Healing

Important Note: Never work directly over any electrical devices such as a pacemaker. Any kind of energy surge could affect the electrical rhythm of the device.

» Next, move your hands so that they are both cupped over and facing toward the center of your chest, held about 3 inches away from the body (not touching).

» State the following divine request: *"I ask Archangel Chamuel to add his divine light to my heart energy center for my greatest and highest good.*" Keep your hands in this position for about two minutes.

Solar Plexus Energy Center

» Next, move your hands so that they both rest directly on your upper stomach area just above the navel (either placed side by side or one above the other).

» State the following divine request: *"I ask Archangel Uriel to add his divine light to my solar plexus energy center for my greatest and highest good."* Keep your hands in this position for about two minutes.

Sacral Plexus Energy Center

» Next, move your hands so that they both rest directly on your lower stomach area just below the navel (either placed side by side or one above the other).

» State the following divine request: *"I ask Archangel Zadkiel to add his divine light to my sacral plexus energy center for my greatest and highest good."* Keep your hands in this position for about two minutes.

Base Energy Center Healing

» Next, move your hands so that they both rest directly on your pelvic and groin area (either placed side by side or one above the other).

» State the following divine request: *"I ask Archangel Gabriel to add his divine light to my base*

energy center for my greatest and highest good."
Keep your hands in this position for about two
minutes.

That's it. You have just given yourself an impressively
powerful divine light healing treatment that can help you
in so many ways. Remove your hands, rub them together,
and shake them off down toward the ground and away
from you. (This will help to shake off any excess energies.)
Thank God and His Archangels for your healing blessings. To help you ground your energies drink a refreshing
glass of water and eat a light snack. Use this exercise daily
or weekly, if you have a serious health issue. Use monthly
or regularly whenever you can to help you improve any
existing health issues and life complaints. The more you
work with divine light, the greater your understanding of
the divine power becomes along with your observation
of the divine healing changes taking place.

Our Body's Energy Pathways

(We can help to get our energies moving.)

*Whereas the seven main energy centers are thought of as
power stations for the body, the meridians can be thought of as
our energetic bloodstream.*

We have the most amazing network of energy channels and pathways that travel deep throughout our entire
body, moving through each of our organs, and carrying a

mixture of electromagnetic energies, subtle energies, and light. These energies and their unrestricted flow through the meridians help to support our organs, tissues, and bodily systems, therefore directly influencing our biological processes. The meridians are most commonly attributed to traditional Chinese medicine, with its complex and extraordinary acupuncture system, dating back thousands of years. A less-invasive way was also developed without the use of acupuncture needles, known as acupressure.

Acupressure points located on the surface of our skin are the energy outlets that connect into and influence the meridian system. Energy traveling through the meridian pathways will often fluctuate due to all kinds of life stressors, and become stagnated, obstructed, congested, or depleted, causing energetic disruptions and jeopardizing our health. Through the use of gentle tapping and massaging, and by holding specific acupressure points located along the surface of the skin, you can instantly help to stimulate, regulate, release, and readjust your energies. In doing so you will begin to maximize a healthy balanced flow and achieve a good energetic rhythm, thereby supporting your health and increasing your vitality. You will discover several easy-to-perform and highly beneficial acupressure techniques in the following chapter to help you instantly manage and boost your vital energies.

Our Subtle Energy Bodies and Energy Fields

(We can empower our soul.)

You have already been introduced to a very important subtle energy body: the etheric subtle body. This is one of seven main subtle energy bodies and energy fields that are protective, reflective, dynamic, and magnetic. All blending and energetically breathing together as an individual unit and expression of our consciousness, they are known in entirety as our bio-auric field. Our subtle energy bodies process many different aspects of us as human souls, so we may build spiritual insight, increase our spiritual power (light), and continuously evolve. We are each a mixture of physical, emotional, psychological, and spiritual energies that are constantly changing. Our bio-auric field is the energetic system that contains our entire spiritual and energetic anatomy—body and soul.

The electrical energy vibration within our auric field is what helps to connect and weave our spiritual and energetic anatomy together. When our electrical energies are balanced, our soul can more easily express its evolved state of divine light (spiritual power) that it has already acquired, so we can begin to co-create our heartfelt dreams and fulfil our life purpose. We can interfere with the electrical energetic connections of our aura, drain our vital life force, and weaken the creative spiritual power of our soul when any aspect of us is consistently out of balance. Our destructive thoughts, our false beliefs, our emotional mood swings, and any toxic behaviors and actions we regularly employ, will knock us out of energetic kilt. It is important to keep a healthy overall balance of each aspect of us, so that we help to keep our energies strong and vibrant.

Our aura is also the buffering system for all of the energies that we regularly encounter on a daily basis within our environment and the atmosphere in which we interact. When the aura is strong and balanced it becomes a wonderful sphere of natural protection against energetic pollution. When the aura is energetically weakened due to any aspect of us being out of balance, it will be less able to do its job of protecting our energies, and we can be left energetically vulnerable. Energetic pollution accounts for all forms of low vibrational toxic energies, which are often covered under the umbrella term *negative energies*. Other people's anger, emotional outbursts, or general negativity can weaken our aura and quickly drain us of our vitality. As can the debilitating effects of florescent lighting, wireless devices, and overhead power lines, to name but a few.

When we have a weakened aura it is less able to process, transmute, and filter out the energetic pollution, and to make use of any enlightened energies we need to support us and our energy systems become easily overwhelmed. Some of our systems will fail to connect with each other as they should due to their messed-up flows and rhythms. We will then lose valuable power in our overall spiritual vibration and our divine light can dim. Our vitality is inevitably drained and this immediately diminishes the power our body needs to stay in healing mode if we become sick. Use the following angel medicine energetic techniques to help you re-establish aura power.

Angel Medicine Aura Power Technique

Use this two-part energetic technique to help you:

» Protect your energies.

» Connect your energies.

» Boost your vitality.

» Increase your soul's ambience and creative power.

Time: approximately 5 to 10 minutes for entire exercise

Part One

» Stand or sit if need be with your hands held in prayer position over the center of your chest to help balance your energies. Take a few deep breaths, in through the nose and out of the mouth, and relax. Stay like this for one minute.

» You are going to create some movement and space within your aura. This is especially helpful if your aura has collapsed closer to your body due to any lack of vibrancy and loss of power. It is an excellent technique for anyone suffering with depression because when a person is depressed his or her energies are always deflated (just like a balloon when it loses its air).

» Begin at the center of your chest and near to the body, but without touching. Use both hands (palms facing you) to make gentle sweeping and rolling movements all across the front of the body, moving from side to side and moving outward as far as you can naturally stretch your arms. You are really helping to fluff the energies of your aura to get them moving.

» Do this exact same routine all the way down to your feet, and then bring your hands back up to the center of your throat area and do the exact same process for the top half of your aura, finishing at the top of your head. Be creative. You cannot do it wrong, as you are creating subtle movements.

Part Two

» With your right hand held out in front of you (palm facing away from you), draw a large figure eight, the height and width of your body from your head to your feet. Do the same with your left hand.

» Next, with your right hand draw a large figure eight, moving sideways across the center and width of your body. Do the same technique with your left hand.

» Now with either hand (your choice), or both, draw mini figure eights with your fingers, anywhere within your aura that you are specifically drawn to. All of these actions will help to weave all of the energies interconnecting within your aura together.

» Finally, with the middle finger of your right hand, hold the brow energy center located between and a little above the eyebrows (with very light pressure). Use the middle finger of your left hand to hold the healing point located just above the navel (with very light pressure). Stay in this position for a few minutes while taking some long, slow, deep breaths. You may feel a warm, burning-like, or hot sensation in your fingertips as you hold these points. This is a good sign, as you will be helping to connect your energies and also bring subtle energy to where it is most needed.

༺◌༻

That's it! Two easy and energetically fantastic techniques to help support your aura protection and regain its healing power.

Our Higher Self

(We can align with the divine.)

Our spiritual connection to God through the Holy Spirit, the Christ consciousness, and our higher self.

Our higher self is the most glorious spiritual aspect of our soul that is in direct alignment with the Holy Spirit and the Christ consciousness. It constantly sends us an energetic stream of spiritual nourishment from these two magnificent divine forces. Our soul *already* contains these divine forces within us, and so these formidable forces help to nourish and support our own portion of divine light. The divine light of our soul is made ever more powerful through our conscious daily alignment with our higher self.

The following higher self exercise is extremely potent in helping you to purposely align with the divine powers of heaven. Your body and soul will be immersed in the white light of the Holy Spirit and will receive the divine light of the Christ consciousness—the most powerful divine light that exists within the heaven realms and in the entire universe, and the most revered by all of the angels. These two ultra-powerful divine forces work in spiritual harmony with the seven divine light frequencies of the holy Archangels. They are extremely important in helping to supply your soul with enough spiritual power to receive, retain, and anchor the potent divine light frequencies of the Archangels, within your energetic anatomy and physical body.

Angel Medicine Higher Self Alignment Exercise

Use this divine exercise to help you:

» Receive spiritual nourishment for your soul.

» Empower your soul to retain and anchor a greater amount of divine light.

» To infuse your cells with the Christ light (placing you in instant healing mode).

Time: approximately 3 to 4 minutes

You can perform this exercise with your eyes opened or closed. All that is needed from you are your imagination, your observation, and your intent. This is what will set in motion the divine alignment with your higher self and the powers of heaven.

» Say the following divine prayer to begin: *"I ask for the white light of the Holy Spirit to surround and protect my body and soul. Thank you, God. Amen" (or "it is done!")!*

» While seated in a chair with your legs uncrossed and your hands resting in your lap with your palms facing upward, imagine a brilliant white cylinder of divine light begin to form all around you.

» Visualize yourself sitting directly in the middle of this beautiful column of white light that stretches far above your head, reaching upward toward the heavens. It also travels several feet into the ground under your feet. You are now totally enveloped and completely immersed in a protective spiritual column of light and divine power. It is the white light of the Holy Spirit. Sitting within this light you will receive immediate spiritual nourishment for your body and soul.

» Next, visualize a flame of intense golden light blazing in the center of your chest and in the area of your heart. Imagine the golden light expanding and growing bigger until soon it has grown much bigger than you. See yourself completely immersed within this golden flame of light. This spiritual process is helping you to expand the power of your soul.

» Next, imagine a brilliant dazzling golden/white ball (think of the sun) of intense bright light shining outward in all directions and elevated several feet directly above your head. *(The exact distance does not matter here. The intention of this step is all that is needed.)* This golden/white light is the divine spiritual power and essence of your higher self.

» Next, imagine your soul's flame of golden light reaching upward to join the very center of your higher self. *(This spiritual step will instantly help you to raise your energy frequency and consciousness to align with the divine power of your higher self.)*

» Next, ask your higher self to transfer the divine light of the Christ consciousness directly into your soul: *"I ask my higher-self to transfer the Christ Light into my soul."* The Christ light can also be perceived as a brilliant golden color. However, the vibrancy of the light cannot be easily expressed, as words are too inadequate to explain how stunningly beautiful it is.

» Observe your soul, your higher self, and the Christ consciousness becoming one big vibrant expanse of dazzling light. You are also still immersed in the white light of the Holy Spirit. You are now completely aligned with the divine powers and forces of heaven.

» State the following three divine affirmations: *"The Christ Light empowers me." "The Christ Light fills every cell of my body." "The white light of the Holy Spirit nourishes and protects me."*

» Finally, bring your awareness back into your heart area, where you will naturally center and balance the added divine power you have attained. Thank God, the Holy Spirit, and the Christ consciousness for your divine blessing.

That's it. This very easy, quick, and extremely powerful divine exercise can help you to achieve outstanding results with your health and within your life with regular use. Each time you use it you will invariably help to increase your spiritual power. Your energy is always changed for the better when you actively choose to align with the divine, as all low vibrational frequencies concerned with illness and disease are transmuted. I cannot recommend this particular exercise enough; it truly is the icing on the cake and the cream of the heavenly crop for all divine healing work.

Chapter 3 will introduce you to an exciting and wonderful mixture of angel medicine exercises and energetic techniques especially formulated to help relieve an array of common complaints.

Chapter Three

Angel Medicine for Common Complaints

The doctor of the future will give no medication, but will interest his patients in the care of the human frame, diet and in the cause and prevention of disease.

—Thomas Edison

In this exciting chapter you will discover a wonderful variety of angel medicine exercises and energetic techniques that are especially customized to help you address and heal an array of the most common health complaints. From headaches and inflammation to general aches and pains, you will be able to take charge of your own energies to help you find a good level of comfort, which can often be instantaneous. They are surprisingly easy to learn and yet they are enormously beneficial in helping you to directly deal with any health challenges you may be experiencing from a spiritual and energetic point of view. When we alter the energetic patterns pertaining to illness, disease, aches, and pains, the vibrational resonance surrounding, interpenetrating, and influencing our organs, systems, and bodily parts will instantly begin to elevate. Our remarkably intelligent bodies can then begin to repair, rejuvenate, and heal.

The Stress Factor

Without a doubt stress is a prevalent factor in the state of our health and well-being. The chemical changes it brings about within the physiology of our body are due to the direct impact stress has within our energy systems. In terms of energetic stress, our energies can become frazzled, sluggish, erratic, and placed into complete disarray. Some systems will begin to swell, congest, leak, and run backward; others are unable to process our energies properly. Our energy systems will therefore be unable to do the specific tasks required of them to help support our entire physical anatomy to keep the body in a healthy state of homeostasis.

We can be physically, emotionally, mentally, and spiritually stressed, and yet continue to ignore our body's signals to re-balance. All of this stress—if not faced, dealt with, and re-balanced—will soon begin to erupt somewhere within our physical body, well-being, and life. The most common physical symptoms due to a buildup of energetic stress within our energetic anatomies cover general health complaints such as insomnia, depression, fatigue, headaches, migraines, blood pressure issues, aches and pains, the common cold, skin complaints, and much more. So many people are habitually drawn to only treating these symptoms instead of dealing with the real core issues, that they continuously live in constant state of stress, moving from one new complaint to another. Whatever you are stressed about needs to be faced, corrected, and balanced, or the symptoms can reappear, or even manifest elsewhere in our bodies as a new complaint.

Our guardian angels are completely aware of the stress we encounter on a daily basis, and how this stress significantly impacts us on all levels. They do what they can to divinely influence us to help us lessen our stress, so that we can regain our life balance and remain vitalized, empowered, and healthy. Our guardian angel will often give us the intuitive nudge to rest and slow down, to go to bed earlier, to spend some alone time, to alter our diet, to drink more water, to exercise, to make peace in any stressful relationships, and to make some space in our busy schedules for some much-needed fun, and so forth. We can, of course, completely dismiss these divine nudges because our free will can easily override them—which it often does, to our own detriment.

When We Don't Have Time to De-Stress

It is vitally important to find time to relax our body and mind so that we regain our mental clarity, stay in emotional balance, and keep our energy levels strong and vibrant. Oftentimes we just don't have the time to relax when we really wish we could because our schedules are completely chaotic. When we keep going and we fail to balance the rigors of daily stress in our lives, our energies will soon become heightened, on edge, alert, and frenzied. Chronic stress will then become a dominant factor within our energetic anatomy due to the constant daily triggers of the body's fight-or-flight response.

Chronic stress is a prominent factor in all illness and disease, and especially with bodily pain. The fantastic news is that we can now do something about it to help relieve our bodies of stress when we are just too busy to take time off to relax. At least this measure can be our saving grace until we can eventually find some extra time for ourselves to do so. Remove the energetic stress from your spiritual and energetic anatomy, and your body will soon thank you by mirroring health and vitality.

Customized Exercises and Techniques for Common Complaints

All of the divine exercises and energetic techniques found within this chapter will help you to naturally and quickly re-establish healing power and move your body back into healing mode. Due to the assistance of the miraculous divine light all of the other energy medicine techniques will become divinely empowered. This can be likened to energy medicine on steroids. You will now explore a dazzling mixture of angel healing, divine affirmations, healing point work, and energy center/subtle body healing work. This marvelous combination will help to restore the body's vital energy flow, which in turn naturally supports the body's robust health and well-being. They will be extremely effective in helping you to manage and relieve stress. And more importantly, they will help to boost the body's immune power to naturally fight off infection and combat illness.

Approximate times are given for each exercise. However, trust your intuitive sense if you feel you need to stay longer or less in any specific exercise or technique that you are especially drawn to. Commitment is also required as one treatment may be enough to bring relief for the likes of headaches, but generally several treatments (a few each day) will be needed to overcome longer-standing symptoms. It is certainly worth the effort if they can help you to achieve complete healing or ease and relieve your complaints. On reading through the clever combination of divine exercises and techniques, you will find that many of them can actually help you with more than one original complaint. They are all especially designed to help ease, relieve, and heal physical symptoms energetically, and by using them you will soon begin to feel de-stressed, more alert, happier, and healthier.

Important Notes When Performing Energy Healing Work

» Never work directly over any electrical devices such as a pacemaker. This is because any kind of energy surge could affect the electrical rhythm of the device. This includes tapping, holding, pressing, and massaging.

» Never tap, press, or massage directly over any bruises, burns, broken or brittle bones, and injuries.

» When you do any kind of energy healing work it is always wise to drink plenty of purified water as this will help to move toxins out of your system. It is also beneficial to keep your body hydrated to support the energy healing work taking place.

Angel Medicine Exercises for Common Complaints

Headaches (Tension)

Use this divine exercise to help you:

» Ease or heal your head pain.

» Balance both hemispheres of your brain to calm an over-analyzing, tense mind.

» Calm your nervous system.

» Ease stress and tension.

» Overcome insomnia.

Total time: approximately 10 minutes

Archangel Healing Power

Ask Archangel Raphael to help release your mental tension and heal your headache. Visualize emerald green light completely surrounding your entire head and neck area while taking a few long, slow, deep breaths. Say: *"Archangel Raphael, please use your divine light to help release my mental tension and heal my headache."* The divine light will now assist you with the following healing techniques.

Healing Points

With your index, middle, and ring fingertips of both hands, hold and massage the acupressure healing points located at the lower back of your head in the indentations where the ridge of your skull meets your neck. (See the illustration.) You will know when you are touching the correct points, as they will sometimes feel quite tender when using moderate to firm pressure. Take a few long, slow, deep breaths in through the nose and out of the mouth, and relax. After you have massaged them a little and they feel less sore, continue to hold these points with light pressure for a minute or so. You may feel a warm, burning-like, or hot sensation in your fingertips as you hold these points. This is a good sign as you will be helping to connect and balance your energies and also bring subtle energy to where it is most needed. You will also help to anchor divine light there so it can begin to work at the deepest levels of your psyche.

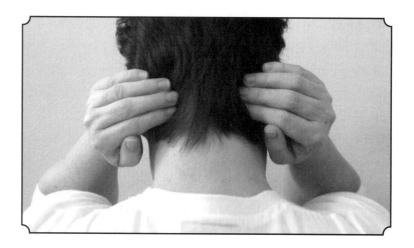

Energy Center/Subtle Body

Place your right palm lightly over your right temple and your left palm lightly over your left temple, keeping all fingers together (no pressure). After a minute or so your hands may begin to feel warm, tingly, or hot as divine light and subtle energies help to balance both hemispheres of the brain. After a few more minutes move your right palm placing it sideways, going across your forehead and place your left palm on the back of your head near your neck, also going sideways in the opposite direction (again, no pressure). Keep your hands in this position for a few minutes until you feel the mental tension melting away. This is an excellent technique to use regularly for easing stress and tension, and especially for helping to overcome any issues of insomnia.

Divine Affirmation

"Divine light clears my tension headache. Divine love heals my tension headache." (You can repeat this divine affirmation over and over, as it will add incredible healing power to where it is most needed.)

Eye Issues (Sore and Tired Eyes) and Ear Issues

Use this divine exercise to help you:

» Ease or heal sore and tired eyes.

» Ease or heal ear issues (earaches, hearing problems).

» Improve foggy vision.

» Relieve hay fever.

» Ease jaw pain (TMJ).

» Ease toothaches.

» Relieve headaches.

» Strengthen your natural intuitive nature.

Total time: approximately 10 minutes

Archangel Healing Power

Ask Archangel Raphael to help heal your tired sore eyes and/or your ear issues. Visualize emerald green light completely surrounding your entire head area, especially over the face, eyes, and ears, while taking a few long, slow, deep breaths. Say: *"Archangel Raphael, please use your divine light to heal my tired sore eyes and/or ear issues."* The divine light will now assist you with the following healing techniques.

Healing Points for the Eyes

With both of your thumbs press with moderate pressure the two healing points located in the indentations under the inner edge of your eyebrows near to the bridge of the nose. Take a few long, slow, deep breaths in through the nose and out of the mouth and relax. Hold these points for about 30 seconds. This is an excellent technique to use regularly for relieving tired eyes, hay fever, headaches, and foggy vision.

Healing Points for the Ears

Use your index, middle, and ring fingertips of both hands to gently place them directly on your face in front of each ear. Hold these points with very light pressure for a few minutes while taking a few long, slow, deep breaths. This is a very easy technique that is extremely beneficial for relieving ear, jaw, and teeth problems. You may feel a warm, burning-like, or hot sensation in your fingertips as you continue to hold these points. This is a good sign, as you will be helping to connect and balance your energies and also bring subtle energy to where it is most needed. You are also anchoring divine light there to help you heal at the deepest level of your psyche.

Energy Center/Subtle Body

With the middle fingertip of your right hand gently hold (very light pressure) the brow energy center point located between and a little above the eyebrows. (This will help to empower the energies that support your eyes). With the palm of your left hand gently lay it (no pressure) directly on your upper stomach area just above the navel in the area of the solar plexus energy center. (Due to the location of both hand and fingertip, it will help to re-balance and align your own personal power with your higher sense perception, so you can improve your intuition at a much deeper level.) Stay in this position for a few minutes while taking some long, slow, deep breaths to relax. You may feel a warm, burning-like, tingling, or hot sensation as you continue to hold these areas. This is a good sign as you will be helping to connect and balance your energies and also bring subtle energy to where it is most needed. You will also help to anchor divine light there so it can begin to work at the deepest levels of your psyche.

Divine Affirmation

"Divine light clears my sore eyes. Divine love heals my sore eyes." "Divine light clears my ear issues. Divine love heals my ear issues." (You can repeat this divine affirmation over and over, as it will add incredible healing power to where it is most needed.)

Sore Throat

Use this divine exercise to help you:

» Ease or heal a sore throat.

» Overcome or relieve an annoying cough.

» Balance and improve any thyroid problems.

» Ease or heal neck pain.

» Speed up healing of tonsillitis.

» Improve the body's metabolic rate.

Total time: approximately 10 minutes

Archangel Healing Power

Ask Archangel Michael to help heal your sore throat. Visualize royal blue light completely surrounding your entire head, throat, and neck area, while taking a few long, slow, deep breaths. Say: *"Archangel Michael, please use your divine light to heal my sore throat."* The divine light will now assist you with the following healing techniques.

Healing Points

Use your index, middle, and ring fingertips to massage or tap the acupressure points known as the K-27 points, with moderate pressure. They are paired energy points located on both sides of the body found just below the collarbone in the small indentations. (See the illustration.) Take a few long, slow, deep breaths as you massage or tap them and relax. Do this for about 30 seconds. Next, continue to hold these points without massaging or tapping them, and with very light pressure, while you move your head slowly to the right as far as you can and bring it back to the center. Then move your head slowly to the left as far as you can and bring it back to the center. Next move your head up toward the heavens and then move it down toward the ground. This wonderful stretching movement will help to free and move any stagnant energies located and stuck within your neck and throat area, while also assisting the subtle energies to flow through your throat and thyroid. Once you have moved in all four directions, you can repeat if necessary, or finish.

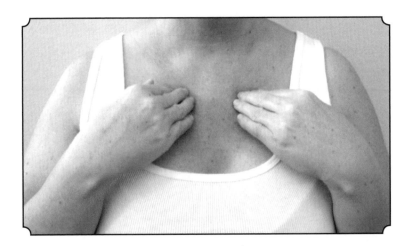

Energy Center/Subtle Body

Place both of your palms directly over and facing the center of your throat and hold approximately 3 inches away from it (not touching). (This will help to empower the energies that support your throat.) Stay in this position for a few minutes, while taking some long, slow, deep breaths to relax. Next, place both of your hands directly on the back of your neck so that your middle fingertips meet each other at the center (no pressure). Stay in this position for a few minutes. You may feel a warm, tingling, or hot sensation in your palms for both hand positions. This is a good sign, as you will be helping to bring subtle energy to where it is most needed. You will also help to anchor divine light there so it can begin to work at the deepest levels of your psyche.

Divine Affirmation

"Divine light clears my sore throat. Divine love heals my sore throat." (You can repeat this divine affirmation over and over, as it will add incredible healing power to where it is most needed.)

Common Cold

Use this divine exercise to help you:

» Speed up your recovery from the cold virus.

» Aid your breathing (asthma issues, lung issues).

» Ease congestion and sinuses.

» Regain your vitality.

» Boost your immune power.

Total time: approximately 10 minutes

Archangel Healing Power

Ask Archangel Chamuel to help release the cold virus from your system. Visualize rose pink light completely surrounding your entire chest area while taking a few long, slow, deep breaths. Say: *"Archangel Chamuel, please use your divine light to help release and heal the cold virus."* The divine light will now assist you with the following healing techniques.

Healing Points

Place the index, middle, and ring fingertips of both hands directly on the thymus healing point, located in the center of your sternum in the bony part of your chest, and begin tapping. Tap in this location for about 20 seconds while taking long, slow, deep breaths, and then stop. This amazing technique will place you into healing mode. (You can also use the K-27 technique you discovered in the previous exercise.)

Next, use the middle fingertips of both hands and place them to the side of each nostril. Place your index fingertips next to them. With moderate pressure gradually press in and upward for 30 seconds. This is a great technique to help you relieve nasal congestion.

Next, use the index, middle, and ring fingertips of both hands to lightly hold the healing points (no pressure) located on the outer side of the chest, near the shoulder area and under the collarbone. Hold these points with very light pressure for a few minutes while taking a few long, slow, deep breaths. You may feel a warm, burning-like, or hot sensation in your fingertips as you continue to hold these points. This is a good sign, as you will be helping to connect and balance your energies, and also bring subtle energy to where it is most needed. You are also anchoring divine light there to help you heal at the deepest level of your psyche. This is a very easy technique that is extremely beneficial for relieving asthma issues, breathing problems, and coughing. I often naturally go to hold these points while taking a bath and relaxing, as they are also excellent points to hold to help re-balance any emotional stress.

Energy Center/Subtle Body

Place both of your palms directly over the center of your chest and hold approximately 3 inches away from it (not touching). (This will help to empower the energies that support your immune system, respiratory system, and circulation system.) Stay in this position for a few minutes, while taking some long, slow, deep breaths to relax. You may feel a warm, tingling, or hot sensation in your palms. This is a good sign, as you will be helping to bring subtle energy to where it is most needed. You will also help to anchor divine light there so it can begin to work at the deepest levels of your psyche.

Divine Affirmation

"Divine light clears my cold virus. Divine love heals my cold." (You can repeat this divine affirmation over and

over, as it will add incredible healing power to where it is most needed.)

Skin Complaints

Use this divine exercise to help you:

» Ease or heal skin complaints.

» Calm your nervous system.

» Ease itching.

» Relieve hives.

» Relieve anxiety.

Total time: approximately 10 minutes

Archangel Healing Power

Ask Archangel Jophiel to help heal your skin complaint. Visualize golden yellow light completely surrounding your skin complaint while taking a few long, slow, deep breaths. Say: *"Archangel Jophiel, please use your divine light to help heal my skin complaint."* The divine light will now assist you with the following healing techniques.

Healing Points

Place the fingertips of both hands to meet directly at the crown of the head. Now, with moderate pressure, drag them across from the center down toward the top of your ears. Bring them back to meet just under the crown, and do this same dragging technique moving out toward the ears. Keep doing this until you have moved down all the way to the nape of your neck. Take your hands back to the crown and do the exact same technique for the front section of the head. (Usually only two movements are required.) Take a few long, slow, deep breaths while doing this. When you have finished, gently tap directly on the crown of your head for about 20 seconds with the fingertips of both hands.

Next, with the middle fingertip of your right hand, gently hold the brow energy center point located between and a little above the eyebrows. (This will help to empower the pituitary gland, which is the master endocrine gland to help support the skin.) Hold this point with very light pressure for a few minutes while taking a few long, slow, deep breaths. You may feel a warm, burning-like, or hot sensation in your fingertips as you continue to hold this point. This is a good sign, as you will be helping to connect and balance your energies and also bring subtle energy to where it is most needed. You are also anchoring divine light there to help you heal at the deepest level of your psyche.

Energy Center/Subtle Body

Place both of your palms directly over the top of your head and hold approximately 3 inches away from it (not touching). (This will help to empower the energies that support your nervous system.) Stay in this position for a few minutes, while taking some long, slow, deep breaths to relax. (It is easier to do this when you are lying down.)

Next, stay in the exact same position, but this time with your palms resting directly on the crown of your head (light pressure). Stay in this position for a few minutes. You may feel a warm, tingling, or hot sensation in your palms for both of these positions. This is a good sign, as you will be helping to bring subtle energy to where it is most needed. You will also help to anchor divine light there so it can begin to work at the deepest levels of your psyche.

Divine Affirmation

"Divine light clears my skin complaints. Divine love heals my skin complaints." (You can repeat this divine affirmation over and over, as it will add incredible healing power to where it is most needed.)

Digestive Problems

Use this divine exercise to help you:

» Ease or heal digestive issues.

» Relieve constipation.

» Relieve an upset tummy.

» Relieve gas and bloating.

» Relieve acid reflux.

Total time: approximately 10 minutes

Archangel Healing Power

Ask Archangel Uriel to help heal your digestive issues. Visualize white/gold light completely surrounding your stomach area while taking a few long, slow, deep breaths. Say: *"Archangel Uriel, please use your divine light to help heal my digestive issues."* The divine light will now assist you with the following healing techniques.

Healing Points

With the index, middle, and ring fingertips of your right hand, very lightly hold the lower stomach healing point located an inch below the navel. With the index, middle, and ring fingertips of your left hand, lightly hold the thymus point in the center of the sternum. (Do not press or massage these points. Simply hold your fingertips there for a few minutes, while taking some long, slow deep breaths to relax.) You may feel a warm, burninglike, or hot sensation as you continue to hold these areas. This is a good sign, as you will be helping to connect and balance your energies and also bring subtle energy to where it is most needed. You will also help to anchor divine light there so it can begin to work at the deepest levels of your psyche.

You will be using your feet for this next great technique. With our without your socks on, use your right heel to massage the healing point located on your left leg below the kneecap and out sideways of the shinbone. (You will know you are on the right spot because it will most likely feel sore to the touch.) Move your heel around for about 30 seconds with moderate pressure to help massage this spot and then change to do the same on the other leg. This is a wonderful technique to help relieve stomachaches and poor digestion.

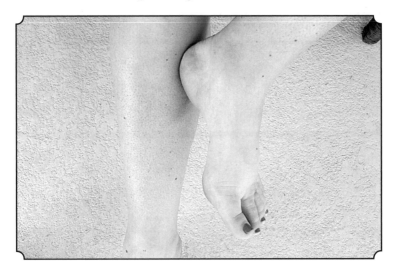

Energy Center/Subtle Body

Place both of your palms directly over the area of your upper stomach just above the navel, and hold approximately 3 inches away from it (not touching). (This will help to empower the energies that support your digestive system.) Stay in this position for a few minutes, while taking some long, slow, deep breaths to relax.

Next, stay in the same position, but this time with your palms lightly resting directly on your stomach just above the navel (no pressure). Stay in this position for a few minutes. You may feel a warm, tingling, or hot sensation in your palms for both positions. This is a good sign, as you will be helping to bring subtle energy to where it is most needed. You will also help to anchor divine light there so it can begin to work at the deepest levels of your psyche.

Divine Affirmation

"Divine light clears my digestive complaints. Divine love heals my digestive complaints." (You can repeat this divine affirmation over and over, as it will add incredible healing power to where it is most needed.)

Aches and Pains (Inflammation)

Use this divine exercise to help you:

» Ease or heal any kind of pain.

» Gain relief from fibromyalgia.

» Ease arthritis pain.

» Ease back pain, hip pain, and sciatica.

» Relieve dizziness.

» Reduce inflammation.

» Increase vitality.

Total time: approximately 10 minutes

Archangel Healing Power

Ask Archangel Zadkiel to help transmute your pain. Visualize violet light completely surrounding and immersing the area of pain while taking a few long, slow, deep breaths. Say: *"Archangel Zadkiel please can you transmute the energetic condition of my painful _____. [Be specific.]"* The divine light will now assist you with the following healing techniques.

Healing Points

To help with pain relief in the upper half of the body, use the middle fingertip of your left hand to lightly hold the healing point located at the lower back of your head in the hollow center of the base of your skull. With the middle fingertip of your right hand lightly hold the brow energy center point located between and a little above the eyebrows. Keep your fingertips in this position for a few minutes while taking some long, slow, deep breaths. You may feel a warm, burning-like, or hot sensation in your fingertips as you continue to hold these points. This is a good sign, as you will be helping to connect and balance your energies and also bring subtle energy to where it is most needed.

To help relieve pain throughout your entire body use the following technique. With your index, middle, and ring fingertips of both hands, lightly hold the healing points located at the lower back of your head in the indentations where the ridge of your skull meets your neck. Take a few long, slow deep breaths in through the nose and out of the mouth, and relax. You may feel a warm, burning-like, or hot sensation in your fingertips as you continue to hold these points. Again, this is a good sign. Not only can the regular use of this excellent technique help to relieve pain in all areas of the body, but it is also great for any coordination problems and dizziness.

To help relieve arthritic pain, gently massage the healing point located on the upside outer edge of the elbow crease with your index, middle, and ring fingertips. (Do both arms one at a time, or cross them over and do both together.) It is easy to find because when you fold your arm you can follow the crease to the outer edge. Do this for 30 seconds while breathing deeply. You will notice when you are on the correct point, as it can feel quite tender.

To help relieve lower back pain, hip pain, and sciatica, place both of your palms directly behind your lower back, so your hands meet at the center of your spine and slightly cover over the top part of your buttocks. Stay in this position for a few minutes, while taking some long, slow, deep breaths. You may feel a warm, tingling, or hot sensation in your palms as you continue to hold this area.

Next, use the middle finger of both hands to press the paired healing points located in the center top half of the buttocks. You will know when you find them because they will feel sore to the touch. Hold them with firm pressure for a few moments and then release. Do this daily to help you get your energies moving.

Energy Center/Subtle Body

Locate the area of pain in your body. You are going to be working directly over the area of pain *without physically touching it* and also with the nearest energy center to the area of pain. First, find the energy center located near to the area of pain. The seven main energy centers are located at the crown, the forehead, the throat, the chest, the upper stomach, the lower stomach, and the pelvis. (See the illustration in Chapter 2.) For any hands, fingers, and arms pain, refer to the chest/heart energy center. For any legs, knees, and feet pain refer to the pelvic/base energy center.

Example: If you have a painful knee, the nearest main energy center will be the pelvic/base center. Start working with the energy center first. Begin to hover the palm of either hand directly over, and hold approximately 3 inches above your groin area (base energy center) and begin moving your hand in a slow, counter-clockwise motion that covers the width of your body. (Imagine your whole body is a clock face with the 12:00 point at your head, and you will know which direction to move your hand.) The counterclockwise movement helps to draw out toxic energies and release stagnant energies from the energy center that keeps inflammation at bay. Move your hand in this direction for a minute or so. Now remove your hand and shake it away from your body, facing down toward the ground to help release any excess energies. Next, use your other hand in exactly the same way, but this time move it in a clockwise direction. This direction will help to re-balance the energy frequencies and flow within the energy center and help to harmonize your energy system. Move your hand in this direction for a minute or so, and then shake off any excess energy down toward the ground.

Now do the exact same technique directly over and above the area of pain in your body (again not touching). If the pain is located at the back of your body, work over the front part of the body that is in direct alignment with the pain. That's it—extremely easy and probably one of the most beneficial energy healing treatments you can do for yourself to instantly help you. Do this exercise daily until you notice the pain has significantly reduced or gone. You will definitely help to speed up the body's healing and repair work.

You can use this exercise on all seven energy centers to help you re-balance your energies and to move life force energy throughout all of your systems, especially if you are suffering with any illness and dis-ease. You never need to touch the body. When doing the entire seven energy centers always begin at the base energy center and finish at the crown energy center. *(For males, when you reach the crown energy center begin by moving in a clockwise motion first, then counterclockwise. This is the only difference required between both sexes.)*

Divine Affirmation

"Divine light clears my pain. Divine love replaces and heals my and pain." (You can repeat this divine affirmation over

and over, as it will add incredible healing power to where it is most needed.)

Fatigue

Use this divine exercise to help you:

» Boost your vitality.

» Improve your memory, focus, and concentration.

» Place yourself back into healing mode.

Time: approximately 10 minutes

Archangel Healing Power

Ask Archangel Gabriel to help you increase your vitality. Visualize white and vibrant orange light completely surrounding and infusing your entire body, while taking a few long, slow, deep breaths. Say: *"Archangel Gabriel, please help to increase my vitality."* The divine light will now assist you with the following healing techniques.

Healing Points

Use your index, middle, and ring fingertips to massage or tap the acupressure points known as the K-27 points, with moderate pressure. They are paired energy points located on both sides of the body found just below the collarbone in the small indentations. Take a few long, slow, deep breaths as you massage or tap them, and relax. Do this for about 30 seconds. This is an excellent technique to help you get your energy circuitry running in the correct direction, because these points influence all of the other energy pathways. They will help to boost your vitality by instantly energizing you until you have more time to rest.

Next, with the middle fingertip of your right hand, gently hold (very light pressure) the brow energy center point, located between and a little above the eyebrows. This potent technique can help to clear mental fatigue, confusion, and irritability.

Energy Center/Subtle Body

Take a few moments to stand outside (it doesn't have to be sunny to work), with your shoes off and your feet in direct contact with the ground. Relax your body and muscles, and stand comfortably with your feet shoulder width apart.

Begin to stretch your arms heavenward with your palms facing toward the sun as you take a few long, slow, deep breaths. You will be stretching your spine and freeing trapped energies. Imagine the life force of the sun rushing into the palms of your hands and entering through the energy center located at the top of your head. Imagine it filling up your entire body with glorious golden yellow light.

Now bring both of your arms back down to your sides, but with your palms facing down toward the ground. Imagine the life force of the earth rushing in through the souls of your feet and into the palms of your hands, filling up your entire body all the way to your head with bril-liant vibrant orange light. Finish by shaking your body, arms, and legs (lifting one leg at a time to shake them). That's it—easy, simple, and all-powerful!

Note: You can do this exact same exercise in the comfort of your own home if you do not wish to do so outside.

Divine Affirmation

"Divine light clears my fatigue. Divine love vitalizes me." (You can repeat this divine affirmation over and over, as it will add incredible healing power to where it is most needed.)

Speed Up the Healing of an Injury and Release Traumatic Memories

Use this divine exercise to help you:

» Repair and heal an injury.

» Process and release fear and the effects of trauma from the cellular memory.

» Release pain and discomfort from any new or old injures.

» Transmute any traumatic memories that still weigh you down emotionally.

Total time: approximately 10 minutes

Note: Always seek medical advice for any injuries and pain. (For any broken bones or fractures, always wait until they have been set and repaired correctly by a surgeon before you begin any energy healing work.)

Five weeks before my wedding day, I slipped when walking down the stairs in my home due to having ice-cold feet and no shoes on. I dislocated my right foot, and fractured and broke my right ankle and leg. My ankle and leg were so badly injured that I needed an emergency operation that same day to fix them. They now hold 10 pins and three plates. I stayed in hospital for four days and was nicknamed the runaway bride because my entire foot, ankle, and leg were in solid plaster right up to my knee, and everyone thought I would need to postpone my wedding. I asked the surgeon who fixed my leg and ankle how long it would take for the plaster to be removed. My honeymoon was already booked to New York the day after my wedding, and there was no way I would be able to fly with plaster on my leg, especially on a nine-hour flight from the UK. I was told that with the injury I had I could reasonably expect to be in plaster for up to seven to eight weeks and that flying with a plaster on was definitely not an option.

What a predicament. I asked for the divine power of God's holy angels to help me. During my meditation I was told by my guardian angel that if I stayed as calm as I could each day (taking me out of stress mode so that the energetic effects of stress didn't interfere with and suppress my healing and recovery) and used daily energy medicine techniques and divine healing work, that I would still marry on the day I had planned and would also go on my honeymoon.

Five weeks later, and just two days before I was scheduled to get married, the surgeon took an x-ray of my ankle and leg and was stunned by the positive results. He gave permission for the plaster to be removed that very day. My guardian angel was right, and I was completely overjoyed. I walked down the aisle on crutches for my wedding day—and I continued on my honeymoon to New York as planned.

Energy healing techniques, divine healing work, and faith in a higher power are what helped me to speed up my own healing. These three superb divine prescriptions worked perfectly in harmony with the surgeon's skilled repair work. The following exercise and techniques are what especially helped me to speed up my healing and repair my injury. If you have any old injures that are still causing you pain and discomfort, then this marvelous exercise will certainly help you.

Archangel Healing Power

Ask Archangel Raphael to help repair your injury and heal any physical pain. Also ask Archangel Zadkiel to transmute any cellular fear associated with your injury. Visualize emerald green light completely surrounding and infusing your entire body as you state the following: *"Archangel Raphael, please help to repair my injury and*

heal my physical pain [be specific with what injury you have]."
Visualize violet light completely surrounding and infusing your entire body as you state the following: *"Archangel Zadkiel, please help to transmute any cellular fear associated with my injury."*

Healing Points

Lightly hold the brow energy center point located between and a little above the eyebrows with the middle fingertip of your right hand, while you also bring to mind and acknowledge the trauma memory and fear associated with your injury. (It is important to bring to mind exactly what you are fearful about to help you clear, balance, and release it from your cellular memory.) Personally, I was afraid of walking down any kind of stairs, due to the cellular memory of my injury being firmly held within my body and mind, and every time I was about to walk down the stairs a fear response would be triggered within my nervous system, keeping me in stress mode. When we are in stress mode we are out of healing mode.

We can still hold the trauma memory of an old accident or incident within our cells without us consciously feeling the fear connected with it, but the response can still be triggered within our nervous system whenever we encounter or hear about a similar situation. This is why healing any old, traumatic memories is also invaluable toward supporting our overall health and well-being.

After a minute or so of keeping your fingertip on your brow energy center point and bringing to mind your trauma memory, make the following statement three times while very gently and lightly tapping the point: *"All of the places in my body, mind, and soul where the anxiety and fear associated with this memory has been stored, are now cleared."* Divine light and subtle energies will begin to assist the brain in making immediate neurological changes.

That's it! This is a very powerful exercise that can be repeated as often as necessary. It will help to revitalize you, empower you, and free you from stress mode so that your body has enough energy (power) to heal and repair.

Energy Center/Subtle Body

Place both palms directly over and hold approximately 3 inches above the area of your body that is injured (not touching). Your hands may begin to feel warm, tingly, or hot after a few moments of doing so. Next, state the following out loud: *"I ask for the white light of the Holy Spirit to help re-pattern my injured _____ [be specific] back to God's original whole divine design of a perfect healthy _____ [be specific]."* I will use my old injury as an example: *"I ask for the white light of the Holy Spirit to help re-pattern my injured leg and ankle back to God's original whole divine design of a perfect healthy leg and ankle."* Keep your hands still and you will more than likely feel a flow of energy taking place. However, it is not necessary to feel anything for the divine restructuring to work. After several minutes you can finish by removing your hands. Thank God, the Holy Spirit, and the Archangels for assisting you. (All of this healing work will help to dramatically reduce the pain and discomfort of your injury as permanent healing changes begins to take root.)

Divine Affirmation

"Divine light clears my cellular fear. Divine love completely heals me." (You can repeat this divine affirmation over and over, as it will add incredible healing power to where it is most needed.)

With your newfound energetic awareness, you can now take active charge of your health issues to help relieve numerous complaints. The next chapter naturally leads us into the deeper aspects of divine healing work through the use of all-powerful divine medicine prayer decrees and exercises. They are uniquely formulated toward correcting any discordant energy patterns within our spiritual and energetic anatomy related to our false beliefs, destructive habits, and behaviors.

Chapter Four

Angel Medicine Prayer Frequencies

The simple act of praying is one of the greatest abilities we have as human souls to help us instantly connect with the divine power to activate spiritual assistance. We are already an integral part of this divine power because the Holy Spirit of God dwells within us, but when we reach out to a higher power—who is much greater than us alone—then we will immediately magnify God's love and healing for our health and our life. The power of prayer is so magnificent, especially if said with an open heart, expectation, faith, and a sincere desire for divine intervention. It is our wonderful guardian angels who take our prayer requests to God to be heard and who deliver God's power back to us in ways that will always be in alignment with our soul's greatest good.

In this chapter you will explore the divine power of prayer and how to pray high vibrational prayers for best results. You will also receive specialized angel medicine prayer frequencies to help you immediately begin to correct, adjust, and repair any discordant patterns of behavior and destructive habits that are too difficult to heal and overcome alone. These all-powerful prayer frequencies will help you to align with divine truth and divine love—removing the error and illusion that interfere with your true divine nature. When the errors and illusions are removed, divine healing power can take root and bring truly remarkable life changes. From this chapter onward we will move into the deeper patterns of healing, so we can really address those pesky issues that hold us back and keep us from shining.

My Own Prayer Experience

I am totally passionate about working with God's holy angels, and this passion came about purely because of the divine power of prayer. I have naturally developed a very close connection to the angelic realm beginning when I was a small child. Beginning at such a tender young age, I have always felt a strong connection to a higher power, and this was certainly strengthened through reciting daily a beautiful prayer I had learned in school, which mentioned the angels: *"Lord, keep us safe this night, secure from all our fears, may angels guard us while we sleep, till morning light appears, Amen."* (John Leland).

This delightful prayer touched my heart and soul, and got me thinking about God's angels and of His love for us so that He would send us His angels to protect us. I also began to recite the prayer every night before my sleep, accompanied by a sincere belief that my prayer was also heard and answered. From this very young age I innocently discovered the divine power of prayer, and I know for sure that it helped me to establish an open line and direct link to the powers of heaven. I soon began to notice and feel the holy angels around myself and others, and I could easily communicate with my guardian angel via my thoughts and receive their divine guidance.

The divine power of prayer is so miraculous that it will enable you to keep in constant contact with God, so that His holy angels can help to divinely guide you, assist you, and bless you in all your ways. This is what co-creation is all about: You admit you cannot do it all on your own, and so you reach out to a higher power for spiritual assistance. You will then become spiritually empowered and receive exactly what you need to make positive and significant life changes. It is a joining of forces—your individual portion of divine design joining with the one divine source of power, so that you will instantly increase and activate your own spiritual power. If you have never, ever prayed, then you really are missing out on so much divine inspiration and guidance, along with the chance of encountering spectacular divine intervention.

Why People Don't Pray

Many people have different reasons for why they don't pray. Here are the four reasons that I hear the most:

>> "I don't believe in God, although I do believe in angels."

>> "Praying is religious and I am not religious."

>> "Prayers don't work."

>> "I don't know how to pray."

"I Don't Believe in God, Although I Do Believe in Angels"

I am amazed when I hear that people don't believe in God, but they do believe in angels. God is the creator of the angels, and therefore the angels wouldn't even exist if it were not for God. The guardian angels will make perfect use of the person's belief in them to help divinely influence them concerning their true divine origin. These glorious angels are truly devoted to God, and they will do whatever they can to help us spiritually awaken. We are never truly separated from God, as this is an impossible task. We can, however, be unconsciously separated because of our false beliefs. All we need to do is correct the false belief and we will consciously align with the divine.

"Praying Is Religious and I Am Not Religious"

Usually a person who associates the divine act of prayer to be religious is simply misguided about prayer and religion. Many people have automatic negative beliefs associated with religion, which is usually due to them accepting other people's beliefs as their own without ever questioning them. Automatic beliefs can be likened to following the herd without ever knowing our own heart, mind, and soul. It is always important to think our own thoughts and to question our beliefs in measurement of divine truth and divine love. Religion, as with anything else, is how we perceive it to be, which angle we choose to look at it, and whether we accept that belief as true for us. If religion is focused on love, peace, and communion with God, then this will be in alignment with divine truth. When religion is used to control, to judge and condemn others, to cause fear, and to place greed and wealth before divine communion, then this is out of alignment with divine truth and divine love.

We need to respect other people's personal paths to God without judgment; this in itself is in alignment with divine love. You do not need to go to church or to be part of any kind of religion to talk to God. You can talk to God anytime and anyplace. Anyone can pray, whether they are religious or not. Prayer is free, and prayer is your own personal connection to the divine powers of heaven.

"Prayers Don't Work"

Many people will claim that prayers don't work because what they have asked God for they didn't receive, and to them this is firm and convincing evidence. This particular reason usually concerns people who are less spiritually mature in understanding God and in understanding their own divine nature. There is nothing wrong with this, of course, if they remain open enough to learn and overcome their misunderstandings. We are all spiritually growing and evolving at different rates, and so there will be a diversity of beliefs spread throughout humanity.

However, if a person stubbornly refuses to spiritually grow, refuses to seek divine truth, and refuses to learn more than what his or her consciousness presently knows, then that person will block her own good and her divine supply. She will continuously keep re-experiencing her life at her current level of consciousness, due to her own false and limiting beliefs—therefore building more so-called firm evidence to back up her own misguided theories. Stubborn pride in our need to be right and in our refusal to change our narrow-minded point of view literally gets us nowhere fast.

Our beliefs and perceptions really do interfere with our divine connection to a higher power, and with all aspects of our health and life. Our dominant thoughts become our beliefs, and our beliefs, whether aligned with divine truth and divine love, or whether out of alignment with divine truth and divine love, *will become our reality.* If we believe prayers don't work, then we will predominantly experience the results of this in our life. You cannot pray and expect your prayers to be answered if you also hold the dual and conflicting belief that prayers don't work and God doesn't listen. A few other reasons for why prayers don't work includes the following:

» **Lack of patience and loss of faith when prayers aren't answered quickly enough.** This kind of attitude will just delay, limit, or completely block the divine power and spiritual assistance to help us. When we are not willing to wait for divine timing, or when we doubt and disbelieve in our prayers being answered, then we will inadvertently hinder them.

» **Laziness, or fear on our part for the necessary actions and life changes we must take in order to receive our heartfelt prayers.** This kind of attitude can interfere with our prayers being answered, or it can be responsible for any missed golden opportunities sent our way.

» **What we have prayed for does not serve our greatest good.** God knows what best serves us, and if what we have asked for dramatically interferes with our life purpose, then it is for our own good that we don't receive it.

» **Feelings of unworthiness and that God has greater things to do than answering our feeble prayers.** God gave us free will, and this includes free will to think, to believe, to feel, to choose, and to act. We must overcome our low self-esteem. God has legions of angels waiting to help us.

If we hold the dominant belief that prayers don't work within our consciousness, then we will also naturally resonate with other false assumptions and beliefs, such as that God doesn't love us and that we are all alone in the world. Depression, loneliness, and unhappiness can result from a deep internal belief that we are separate from God. Long-term thinking and feeling in this way will inevitability alter our physiology, and our health and well-being will begin to suffer. These false beliefs can also be unconscious within our energy systems, especially if we have had many prior experiences of so-called failed prayers. In other words, we may strongly believe in God, but at an unconscious level we will also hold the false belief that prayers don't work. (Use the divine medicine separation exercise later in this chapter to immediately help you correct these false and limiting beliefs.)

We have many conscious and unconscious beliefs that do not align with divine truth and divine love, because we all have free will to think, accept, and believe what we want. If you don't like what you see in your own life, then you need to use your free will to change your thought patterns and beliefs. Alter your thinking, correct your false beliefs, and—wow—you have a divine prescription for success! You will soon see desirable results manifesting in your health and life. I can attest that being in alignment with divine truth and divine love will be far more beneficial to you for the rest of your life, then sticking with your old, false, limiting, and self-destructive beliefs.

"I Don't Know How to Pray"

This reason is typically given or is too easily used as an excuse for not praying. Just because we do not know how to do something, does not mean we should completely give up without ever trying again. The guardian angels take our prayers to God, and *any prayers* we pray that are sincere and said with an open heart are definitely going to be heard. Combining these ingredients with the spiritual power of divine expectation, hope, and faith in God will set our prayers apart from those of others, who recite their prayers with no real divine feeling. In other words, if you are repeating the divine affirmation *"Divine love heals me"* over and over, while at the same time you are also thinking of what's for dinner later that night, then your prayers will lack divine healing power. They can still work, but not as potently as they could.

Over the years I have come to learn so much about prayers because I have prayed daily ever since I was a very small child, and as I matured, so did my prayers and my spiritual understanding mature. The angels have taught me all about different kinds of prayers and their divine powers through my meditations to align with the divine. Following is some invaluable divine advice from the angels regarding how to pray:

» **Talk to God as you would talk to a best friend.** Talk naturally and express our real feelings. God is listening to us.

» **Know that we are worthy.** If we think and believe that we are not worthy of God's love, then our prayers will lose some of their divine potency.

» **Stay in faith.** If we pray without divine feeling, expectation, and faith, then our prayers will lack divine power.

» **Pray daily and especially when we need help.** If we don't pray when we really do need help, then we can miss out on the most wonderful divine intervention and life blessings.

» **Pray for joy, health, happiness, and divine protection for others.** When we pray for others it must be to allow God to work within that person's life, not for us to try to manipulate the changes we would particularly want for that person's life. (We must get out of the way.) Otherwise, our prayers will lack divine power.

Finally, the most powerful prayers I have been taught by the angels are prayers of correction and prayers of thanksgiving. You will discover more about prayers of correction shortly as this is what will especially help to bring you into deeper levels of healing.

Prayers of Thanksgiving

Prayers of thanksgiving help to release astonishing amounts of divine power if said with real sincerity and the adjoined feelings of our heart and soul. They begin to create positive, subtle shifts in our spiritual and energetic anatomy and our life so that over time we begin to notice that we are naturally happier, healthier, and more and fulfilled. Use the following divine prayers of thanksgiving as examples for you to begin to pray over anything and everything important in your life and soon you will be absolutely astounded by the results:

» "Thank you, God, for my health."

» "Thank you, God, for my life."

» "Thank you, God, for my husband/wife."

» "Thank you, God, for my family, my home, my work, my career."

» "Thank you, God, for my friends."

» "Thank you, God, for your blessings and favor in my life."

» "Thank you, God, for my guardian angel."

One powerful thanksgiving prayer that I personally say daily is this very special one: *"I love you God. I love my life. Thank you, God."* I say it with divine feeling and meaning, and it absolutely keeps me closely aligned with the divine power.

Never underestimate the divine power of prayer. God *will* move mountains just for you. You must find your own special way to pray. You can pray anytime of the day or night and for as long as is required. If you begin to pray daily with divine feeling and meaning, then you will naturally continue to mature your prayer life and evolve your soul. You will also deepen your unique conscious connection to God.

During the writing of this particular chapter about divine prayer frequencies, I received an e-mail from a gentleman who liked my Website and who thanked me for the divine healing work I do. He wanted to give me a beautiful divine healing prayer. I have included it here due to the divine coincidence, which as we all know there are no real coincidences. It was meant to be.

Thy name is my healing, O my God, and remembrance of Thee is my remedy. Nearness to Thee is my hope, and love for Thee is my companion. Thy mercy to me is my healing and my succor in both this world and the world to come. Thou, verily, art the All-Bountiful, the All-Knowing, the All-Wise.

$\mathcal{A}$ngel Medicine Prayer Frequencies

Angel medicine prayer frequencies are specially constructed prayers that help to activate immediate divine healing power and are used to correct anything within us that is out of alignment with divine truth and divine love. These prayers of correction help to deeply repair and adjust our discordant energy patterns and frequencies, so that we can move back into divine harmony and align with our true divine origin and our original divine design—helping both body and soul. They help to override our old, erroneous thinking and will begin to transmute our limiting and false beliefs, while also replacing them with their corrections in divine truth and divine love.

You will notice that these prayers do not address any actual dysfunctional behaviors, health issues, or complaints, as they formulated to address the real core issues and the predominant beliefs *found behind our problems.* Use the following extremely important prayers of correction to help you dramatically shift any discordant energies and elevate your entire overall consciousness. Do not underestimate the divine healing power released by these potent prayer frequencies because of their simplicity. The following prayer is definitely the most important of them all with regard to helping us on all levels of our being and in every single aspect and area of our health and our life.

Angel Medicine Prayer for Our False Belief in Being Separate From God

Use this divine exercise to help you:

» Improve or heal depression and psychological disorders.

» Improve or heal all illness and disease.

» Overcome destructive habits, behaviors, and addictions.

» Align with the divine.

» Overcome loneliness, despair, suicidal thoughts, and escapism.

» Re-establish your divine creative power.

Time: approximately 1 minute

"Dear God, I am willing to change the false conscious or unconscious patterns held within me that believe I am separate from you. I ask that you correct, repair, heal, and replace this false belief in alignment with divine truth and divine love. I ask that my heart and soul align together with my true divine origin. By the power of your divine light, thank you, God. Amen. It is done!"

Affirm throughout the day: *"I am aligned with the divine."*

This phenomenal divine prayer frequency will set in motion astonishingly powerful alterations within your spiritual and energetic anatomy, which will change your overall consciousness, and positively alter your physiology and biology. You can say this prayer daily until you witness the incredible results of increasing joy, happiness, vibrancy, and renewed health showing up within your life.

Angel Medicine Prayer for Our False Belief That We Are Un-Loveable

Use this divine exercise to help you:

» Improve or heal any illness or disease.

» Improve or heal depression.

» Align with your divine origin.

» Clear the destructive pattern of self-loathing from your consciousness.

» Accept yourself.

Time: approximately 1 minute

"Dear God, I am willing to change the false conscious or unconscious patterns held within me that believes I am un-loveable. I ask that you correct, repair, heal, and replace my false belief in alignment with divine truth and divine love. I ask that my heart and soul align together with my true divine origin. By the power of your divine light, thank you, God. Amen. It is done!"

Affirm throughout the day: *"I am loveable."*

"I love and accept myself."

This specific divine prayer frequency will certainly help with the healing process by placing you back into healing mode. You can say this prayer daily until you witness the incredible results of increasing joy, happiness, vibrancy, and renewed health in your life. It is especially helpful to say this prayer anytime you are actually experiencing intense feelings of being unlovable or of self-loathing, while also repeating the divine affirmation over and over. You will be clearing all these old false limiting thoughts, beliefs, and emotions out of your consciousness for good, so that eventually the day will come when you will notice that you are no longer plagued by them.

Angel Medicine Prayer for Our False Belief That We Are Being Punished by God

Use this divine exercise to help you:

» Improve or heal any illness and disease.

» Overcome destructive habits, behaviors, and addictions.

» Align with your divine origin.

» Clear the destructive pattern of self-sabotage from your consciousness.

Time: approximately 1 minute

"Dear God, I am willing to change the false conscious or unconscious patterns held within me that believe I am being punished by you. I ask that you correct, repair, heal, and replace my false belief in alignment with divine truth and divine love.

I ask that my heart and soul align together with my true divine origin. By the power of your divine light, thank you, God. Amen. It is done!"

Affirm throughout the day: *"God loves me unconditionally."*

This specific divine prayer frequency will certainly help with the healing process by removing the false and limiting beliefs that you are unloved and are being punished by God. This divine correction and removal will prevent you from continuously sabotaging your health and well-being. You can say this prayer daily until you witness the incredible results of increasing joy, happiness, vibrancy, and renewed health showing up within your life.

Angel Medicine Prayer for Our False Belief That We Are Fearful

Use this divine exercise to help you:

» Improve or heal depression.

» Improve or heal any illness and disease.

» Align with our divine origin.

» Overcome destructive habits, behaviors, and addictions.

» Empower every cell in our body with divine love.

Time: approximately 1 minute

"Dear God, I am willing to change the false conscious or unconscious patterns held within me that believe I am irrationally fearful. I ask that you correct, repair, heal, and replace my false belief in alignment with divine truth and divine love. I ask that my heart and soul align together with my true divine origin. By the power of your divine light, thank you, God. Amen. It is done!"

Affirm throughout the day: *"I am powerful beyond measure." "Divine love empowers me."*

This specific divine prayer frequency will certainly help with the healing process by removing the false and limiting belief that you are fearful, which is toxic to your physiology, and can prevent, delay, or limit your healing. This divine correction and removal will prevent you from living in irrational fear about your health, well-being, and life. You can say this prayer daily until you witness the incredible results of increasing joy, happiness, vibrancy, and renewed health showing up within your life.

Angel Medicine Prayer for Our False Belief That We Are Unable to Heal

Use this divine exercise to help you:

- » Improve or heal all illness and disease.

- » Align with your divine origin.

- » Overcome destructive habits, behaviors, and addictions.

- » Shift your perception and increase your faith.

Time: approximately 1 minute

"Dear God, I am willing to change the false conscious or unconscious patterns held within me that believe I am unable to heal. I ask that you correct, repair, heal, and replace my false belief in alignment with divine truth and divine love. I ask that my heart and soul align together with my true divine origin. By the power of your divine light, thank you, God. Amen. It is done!"

Affirm throughout the day: *"Divine love heals me."*

This specific divine prayer frequency will certainly help with the healing process by removing the false and limiting belief that you are unable to heal. This divine correction and removal will also prevent you from continuously sabotaging your health and well-being. You may find that after saying this angel medicine prayer for a certain period of time that you will also begin to respond well to medical treatment, whereas before it would never work for you. You can say this prayer daily until you witness the incredible results of increasing joy, happiness, vibrancy, and renewed health showing up within your life.

*D*ivine Healing Feelings

Divine healing feelings are an absolute necessity in helping to support the natural healing process of the physical body. These marvelous feelings are divine expressions of God's power and love. Divine healing feelings are associated with our original divine origin and include the true radiant joy of our soul. Many of us don't feel these natural divine feelings anymore because we have automatically numbed the expression of our heart and soul due to our painful traumatic experiences. We have forgotten what it actually feels like to *truly feel,* and to express a divine range and variety of healthy emotions. We have forgotten how to live our soul's truth and follow our heart.

We Have Forgotten How to Feel

To numb and prevent our emotional pain from resurfacing we have built an energetic wall (electromagnetic force field) around our heart. This energetic wall is real, and it is meant to keep us safe from being emotionally hurt again. However, living without ever openly feeling our feelings due to our fear of being hurt is to not live up to our full radiant joy and creative potential. We cannot experience the deepest joy of our soul and the greatest love of our soul when our heart energy is blocked from flowing outward into the world to give and receive both joy and love.

Our refusal to overcome, let go of, and move on from past traumas—no matter how minor or major—will often lead to us ignoring our heartfelt desires, sabotaging our happiness, and choosing numerous inappropriate ways to trick ourselves into feeling satisfied, relaxed, and happy. We use these lower-level feelings in an attempt to match them with the true radiant joy of our soul and as a way to try to re-experience our true divine origin, but they are not real. These inappropriate ways often include our free will's role in forming any destructive habits, behaviors, and addictions of all kinds. Symptoms of our blocked heart and soul energy include:

› **Mood swings and emotional sensitivity**—happy one moment and deflated the next. It is our inability to sustain being truly joyful the majority of the time because we rely on other people, circumstances, and things to be solely responsible for our happiness. Being joyful most of the time is completely rational and is not irrational as you may first believe due to the pressures of life. It is rational because joy is associated with our true divine nature. This doesn't mean that we will never encounter another challenging situation to overcome. It simply means that we will choose to not let life circumstances, other people, and things become the controlling factor of our levels of joy. We can then remain in joy or very quickly re-establish our joy when we let go, and move on and remember who we really are.

› **Addictions of all kinds.** This is an attempt to try to re-experience the true joy of the soul through destructive uses, to help us feel satisfied, relaxed, and happy. It is also an attempt to suppress our heart and soul energy as a form of protection, due to the fear of re-experiencing any new pain. (Addictions, destructive behaviors, and habits are typically rooted in our false unconscious or conscious belief that we are separate from God.)

> **Suppressed creativity.** This is because we are stopping our soul power (consciousness) from moving outward into the world to truly live and co-create our lives in accordance with divine truth and divine love. (Abundance issues are associated with blocked heart and soul energy.)

> **Blocked love.** This is because we are afraid of being hurt and re-experiencing our old pain. We will sabotage new relationships or repel anyone from coming too close. At the very least, if we do manage to attract love, and we haven't healed our hurt past, then we can re-experience the exact same old repeated relationship problems over again, therefore reinforcing our need to block our heart.

> **Physiological changes in our body:** immune system suppression, blood pressure issues, hormonal issues, headaches, aches, and pain. This list is pretty endless. Why? Because we refuse to live from our heart and soul. We exist living our lives with a limiting attitude of *this is as good as it gets*. When we stop feeling, we stop living. The big question then is: **How do you feel?** Read through the following list and contemplate your answers.

› **How do you feel?**

» **Do you feel truly happy?** If not, why not?

» **Do you feel compassionate toward yourself and others?** If not, why not?

» **Do you feel peaceful?** If not, why not?

» **Do you feel joyful?** If not, why not?

» **Do you feel creative?** If not, why not?

» **Do you feel trustful?** If not, why not?

» **Do you feel fearless and courageous?** If not, why not?

» **Do you feel abundant?** If not, why not?

» **Do you feel safe and free?** If not, why not?

These questions are provided to help you search your soul for answers. In a quiet moment ask yourself these questions and contemplate the answers that surface within your conscious mind. You will quite likely uncover many limiting thoughts and false beliefs that do not agree with divine truth and divine love in your soul searching.

Many people will claim they are too busy, are under too much pressure, have ongoing financial burdens, and are too ill for them to feel happy, peaceful, fearless, and free, and so forth, without ever realizing that all of these divine feelings are personal choices, and they are a natural aspect of who we really are. The following remarkable angel medicine prayers will help you to download and receive seven all-powerful divine healing feelings directly into your body and soul.

Seven All-Powerful Divine Healing Feelings

The stunning impact that being joyful and happy has on our health is truly enormous and it certainly helps toward us achieving longevity. Joy is therefore one of the seven remarkable divine healing feelings that we can receive direct from God and downloaded into our cells via one of the seven magnificent Archangels. The other six divine healing feelings are courage, wisdom, compassion, abundance, peace, and divine freedom. Receiving these divine healing feelings will help us to align with our true divine nature, so that eventually we can expand them within our soul so that they become our dominant and natural state of being. All seven divine healing feelings are extremely important for the healthy integration of our body, mind, and soul so that we can live our life to the fullest.

Angel Medicine Prayer for Divine Courage With Archangel Michael

"Archangel Michael, I ask to receive the divine healing feeling of courage within every cell of my body, so that my mind, body, and soul resonate with divine courage, strength and

fortitude. Thank you, God. Thank you, Archangel Michael. Amen. It is done!"

Affirm throughout the day: *"My true divine nature is courageous"* and/or *"My true divine nature is fearless."*

Angel Medicine Prayer for Divine Wisdom With Archangel Jophiel

"Archangel Jophiel, I ask to receive the divine healing feeling of wisdom within every cell of my body, so that my mind, body, and soul resonate with divine wisdom. Thank you, God. Thank you, Archangel Jophiel. Amen. It is done!"

Affirm throughout the day: *"My true divine nature is wise."*

Angel Medicine Prayer for Divine Compassion With Archangel Chamuel

"Archangel Chamuel, I ask to receive the divine healing feeling of compassion in every cell of my body, so that my mind, body, and soul resonate with compassion and unconditional love. Thank you, God. Thank you, Archangel Chamuel. Amen. It is done!"

Affirm throughout the day: *"My true divine nature is compassionate."*

Angel Medicine Prayer for Divine Joy With Archangel Gabriel

"Archangel Gabriel, I ask to receive the divine healing feeling of radiant joy in every cell of my body, so that my mind,

body, and soul resonate with radiant joy. Thank you, God. Thank you, Archangel Gabriel. Amen. It is done!"

Affirm throughout the day: *"My true divine nature is radiant joy."*

Angel Medicine Prayer for Divine Abundance With Archangel Raphael

"Archangel Raphael, I ask to receive the divine healing feeling of abundance in every cell of my body, so that my mind, body, and soul resonate with divine abundance. Thank you, God. Thank you, Archangel Raphael. Amen. It is done!"

Affirm throughout the day: *"My true divine nature is abundant."*

Angel Medicine Prayer for Divine Peace With Archangel Uriel

"Archangel Uriel, I ask to receive the divine healing feeling of peace within every cell of my body, so that my mind, body, and soul resonate with divine peace. Thank you, God. Thank you, Archangel Uriel. Amen. It is done!"

Affirm throughout the day: *"My true divine nature is peace."*

Angel Medicine Prayer for Divine Freedom With Archangel Zadkiel

"Archangel Zadkiel, I ask to receive the divine healing feeling of freedom within every cell of my body, so that my mind, body, and soul resonate with divine freedom. Thank you, God. Thank you, Archangel Zadkiel. Amen. It is done!"

Affirm throughout the day: *"My true divine nature is free."*

You are now ready to explore the deeper patterns of healing with the wonderful angel healing experts to help release any karmic patterns of energy that interfere with your health and happiness. Join me now in Chapter 5, in which you will meet and work with these spectacular celestial healers.

Chapter Five

❧

Angel Medicine for Deep Healing Work

Sometimes our health issues will continuously persist no matter how well we are medically examined and treated. No matter how consistent we are with our divine affirmations and energy healing work. And, no matter how often we sincerely pray for our healing. When health issues persist and there are no tangible reasons in this life for why they do, then we need to look in a completely different direction for the deeper reasons and answers pertaining to our bodily complaints. This new direction involves working with our spiritual DNA, which contains all of our evolutionary karma from the time we became an individualized created soul.

This crucially important chapter covers the deepest aspects of divine healing work with the tremendous and all-powerful angel healing experts. These extraordinary divine healers can help us to resolve any evolutionary karma we hold within our spiritual DNA, pertaining to our current state of health and well-being. We can then achieve a greater level of relief and comfort within our daily lives, as our bodies can finally begin to repair and heal from the complaints that have continued to persist.

This exciting chapter also covers divine healing work with the almighty protective force of Archangel Michael for any spiritual concerns you may have regarding the removal of any interfering wayward spirits—known to many people as spiritual warfare. You will find out about the superb angelic surgeons, who work under the majestic charge of the seven mighty Archangels. These incredible angelic surgeons are able to remove energetic anomalies, *and* fix and repair any deep spiritual dysfunctions within our spiritual and energetic anatomy. Finally, you will be given an amazing angel medicine exercise that is completely focused on healing your etheric subtle energy body. This particular exercise can help to create immediate positive physiological responses within our body, so that we can begin to feel instantly calmer and energized. It is one of the most important angel medicine exercises that you can do for yourself to help you clear, re-balance, and recharge your energies, support your immune system, and shift your body back into healing mode.

Our Spiritual DNA

We need to take our soul's energy frequency back to our original divine origin in order for us to resolve and repair any persistent health issues.

Our spiritual DNA is concerned with our divine makeup, structure, and form (spirit and soul), and just like our physical DNA contains our body's genes, our spiritual DNA contains God's divine essence. This is God's divine spark, spirit, and power infused within every mysterious cell of our soul's DNA. We are God's awe-inspired creation, and our souls were made to be whole, perfect, and divine. When our soul and physical body merged together, God's divine force became activated within every cell of our physical body. This is what sustains our consciousness and gives life to our physical form.

We will always hold the divine spark of God within our physical cells during our lifetime. However, we can dim the light and strength of our divine heritage through our errors and our forgetfulness. When our cells are dimmed of divine light and are weakened of the divine force, we can become vulnerable to illness and disease. The divine secret of health and well-being is to therefore align our consciousness with divine truth and divine love, and to correct and resolve any errors that interfere with our natural divine origin. Our physical and spiritual cells can then unite powerfully together as one. This divine process switches on the power contained within our spiritual DNA, to animate and empower every cell in our body with God's divine force. We then move directly into healing mode.

*O*ur Soul Line

For whatever reason, and known only to God, we became human souls without any conscious memory of our divinity. The unconscious memory of our divinity is always retained in our spiritual DNA. From this initial beginning as human souls, and without any conscious memory of our divinity, we made many so-called mistakes—although in the greater spiritual sense, there are no mistakes, only numerous levels of experiencing, learning, and remembering. There must be a divine purpose to this, but again this is not necessarily important for us to know. It is God's divine plan and God knows best.

From us observing throughout the world the many differences found in humanity's life experiences and overall spiritual levels of maturity, it is plain to see that *we* as human souls all exist at different stages of conscious evolution. In this sense, not only does the physical body continuously evolve, but so does the spiritual body continuously evolve. As souls, we do not know how old we truly are while we are human and living a physical life existence. We will know this truth when we exit this life and go on to the heaven realms.

This concept of us existing prior to our human body can be hard for many people to accept because it naturally leads us to question whether or not we have lived before. It is misguided to think that our consciousness has only existed since we were born into a physical body.

God does not play dice with our lives, and neither does He have any favorites. God would not bless one of us with health and wealth, while another one he favors less gets poverty and abuse. God loves us unconditionally and equally. There are greater spiritual reasons and answers pertaining to the *why's* that will be revealed and remembered by us as souls, within the heaven realms.

Whether our soul actually reincarnates to this life in a new body, or whether it carries on having more soul life experiences in other worlds, no one truly knows. One possible theory concerning the belief in reincarnation is that it could simply be the passing along of our ancestors' memories through our physical and spiritual DNA. We could then naturally assume and believe that these memories are our own and that we must have therefore experienced a prior lifetime. In this sense, though, it is evolutionary memories that are carried forward. It is quite possible when going along with this line of thinking that not only are we responsible for *our actions* within this lifetime (the positive use or misuse of our energy), but we may also be responsible for resolving our ancestor's misuse of energy. As previously mentioned, no one truly knows until we move on to the heaven worlds.

Evolutionary Karma

God initially created us as perfect and whole souls, yet we have naturally incurred karma due to our evolutionary process and experiences. The divine law of karma can be more easily defined as the spiritual process of cause and effect. We are obliged to work through our evolutionary karma to help us rebalance our soul's innate spiritual power. With this understanding it is certainly not found to be any kind of punishment, but serves as a divine and perfect measurement of our soul's history and growth. If you perceive it to be payback and punishment, then you are observing it from the least-spiritual point of view and understanding.

Our soul is accountable for whatever energy we give out, positive or negative. We will always have the opportunity to resolve our unbalanced evolutionary karma and spiritually grow. Within this life we have both our karmic history to contend with that we bring forward to this lifetime to resolve, and we also have any new karma being created within this lifetime from any misuse of our energy. Both kinds of karma can and will drastically interfere with our present state of health, happiness, and life circumstances.

You do not have to believe in past lives, ancestor memories, soul history, or even other worlds for the two upcoming angel medicine exercises to work. If you have any health issues that continuously persist and you have tried every other avenue and option of possible help that you can think of, then it is certainly beneficial for you to give them a try, as you have nothing to lose and everything to gain. All that is required are your willingness to forgive, to resolve any soul errors, and to let go, heal, and move on.

Forgive Who?
Forgive Our Past

Forgive yourself for any guilt you still carry within your soul due to any suffering you may have caused to another soul or souls. And forgive others for any suffering and deep pain they have caused you. This is much easier to do for our soul history, as we have no consciousness awareness of it, yet it is still carried deep within our spiritual DNA, and it does interfere with our present health and life issues until it is eventually resolved.

Forgive Our Present

It is of course much harder to forgive those who have caused us to suffer in this lifetime, and to forgive ourselves for any pain we have caused, because we are fully aware and conscious of the experience. Our anger and hatred may be preventing us from forgiving the unforgivable. And our overwhelming guilt may be preventing us from forgiving ourselves. Yet this is an invaluable and necessary step we need to take in order to resolve the new karma that keeps us tied to others and to certain situations. The divine act of forgiveness affords us the greatest healing and freedom we can ever hope to receive. Jesus Christ forgave, and we are meant to follow in His footsteps. We can lean on the power of the Christ consciousness and God's holy angels to help us forgive what we find too difficult to do alone. Deep hatred, anger, guilt, and resentment are extremely detrimental to our health.

Forgiveness does not wipe clean the other person's karma, for he will still need to account for what he did with his misuse of energy, and this is between him and God. The divine act of forgiveness resolves and releases you from that person's energy, so that you can be free to live again with increased spiritual power.

The following two specialized angel medicine exercises will help you to resolve and re-balance the evolutionary karma of your soul. The first divine exercise is concerned with your soul history. The second divine exercise is concerned with this lifetime. This type of deeper healing work will enable you to do a major overhaul within your entire spiritual vibration, increasing the light in and of your soul, and maximizing your divine power and potential. You will then begin to heal those pesky health issues that continuously persist, so that you can completely reinvent yourself, your health, and your life in accordance with greater vibrancy, joy, and success.

Angel Medicine Exercise for Soul History Transmutation and Freedom

Use this divine exercise to help you:

» Resolve and re-balance the evolutionary karma of your soul's history (pertaining to this life).

» Align with your soul's original divine origin.

» Move your body back into healing mode.

» Gain spiritual and physical freedom.

Time: approximately 5 minutes

Divine prayer of surrender

"Dear God, I am willing to resolve my soul's evolutionary errors that currently interferes with my health and life now. I therefore choose to forgive myself and all others for any hurt, suffering, and pain caused within all directions of space and time. I ask that this be for the greatest and highest good of all and for my soul to be restored whole through the Christ consciousness. Thy will be done. Thank you, God. Amen!" This prayer will now serve you through the rest of the exercise.

Archangel power

Sit comfortably and visualize the following: The whole room you are in begins to fill up with violet light. This is the divine light of Archangel Zadkiel. With your wonderful imagination begin to visualize the most glorious Archangel with huge violet wings. Archangel Zadkiel is now with you. All you need to do is to imagine this splendid Archangel standing behind you and placing his hands on your shoulders as you state the following request: *"Archangel Zadkiel, please transmute any painful soul history memories within my spiritual DNA, that interfere with my present health and life circumstances."*

Breathe deeply in a meditative and calm state as you witness this impressive Archangel folding his huge violet wings around your entire body. You may feel an energy surge, you may feel emotional, you may feel heat, or you may feel nothing at all. Just go with this divine exercise and accept the most wonderful divine healing power sent to help you.

That's it! After a few minutes finish by stating the following: *"Thank you, God. Thank you, Archangel Zadkiel. Amen. It is done!"*

Use this angel medicine exercise daily, weekly, or as necessary, until you notice your health and life issues have positively improved.

Angel Medicine Exercise for Resolving Present Life Karma

Use this divine exercise to help you:

» Resolve and re-balance any newly created karma.

» Free yourself from any guilt you carry.

» Move your body back into healing mode.

» Align with your soul's original divine design.

» Gain spiritual and physical freedom.

Time: approximately 5–10 minutes

Divine prayer of surrender

"Dear God, I am willing to resolve my soul's karma pertaining to this life that currently interferes with my health and life now. I therefore choose to forgive myself and all others for any hurt, suffering, and pain caused within my past, present, and future time line. I ask that this be for the greatest and highest good of all and for my soul to be restored whole through the Christ consciousness. Thy will be done. Thank you, God. Amen!"

Archangel power

Sit comfortably and visualize the following: You are seated in a spectacular healing chamber of divine light that exists within the heaven realms. Use your imagination to create the most beautiful room. Your soul is able to visit this special healing sanctuary any time you choose to receive divine healing power and rejuvenation. Today you are here to receive powerful divine healing from Archangel Zadkiel and the Christ Light to free you of your traumatic memories, guilt, and shame—plus, to help you forgive when you find it much too difficult to do so alone.

To free you of traumatic memories: Imagine sitting in a seat of golden light directly under a waterfall of white light (not water), and state the following: *"Archangel Zadkiel, please free me of my painful memory or memories of my traumatic life experience (or _____ [be specific]). I ask that this divine healing move through all of my energy systems* *releasing any and all guilt, pain, and shame that I may carry. Please, heal all of the cellular damage that has been done and bring this healing change into the present moment now. Thank you, God. Thank you, Archangel Zadkiel. Amen. It is done!"* Now imagine violet light pouring from the waterfall all over you. The violet light is washing away and transmuting all of your pain.

To help you forgive: Imagine sitting in a seat of golden light directly under a waterfall of white light (not water), and state the following: *"Archangel Zadkiel, please help me to forgive _____ [say his or her name] for the deep pain and hurt they have caused me. I ask to be free of their energy and that your divine healing move through all of my energy systems releasing any and all anger and hatred I carry toward them. I forgive them. I forgive them. I forgive them. Please, heal all of the cellular damage that has been done and bring this healing change into the present moment now. Thank you, God. Thank you, Archangel Zadkiel. Amen. It is done!"* Now imagine violet light pouring from the waterfall all over you. The violet light is transforming your energy and is freeing your soul connection to this person.

To receive the Christ Light, state the following: *"I ask for the divine healing power of the Holy and magnificent Christ Light to help me in my process of forgiveness as I find it too difficult to do so alone. Thank you, Jesus. Amen. It is done!"*

Divine affirmation

"The power of the Christ Light enables me to forgive."

Use this angel medicine exercise daily, weekly, or as necessary, until you notice your health and life issues have positively improved. You will begin to notice that any memories concerning your painful past will not hurt you as they once did. You will also notice that you are eventually able to forgive. You will then know that you are spiritually free.

Archangel Michael

Sometimes our persistent health issues can be associated with what is known as spiritual warfare. We can be under attack from unseen psychic and spiritual forces that interfere with our state of mind, therefore affecting our health and well-being. Of all the Archangels within the heavenly realms, it is the magnificently powerful Archangel Michael who can best help to free us.

I am not Catholic, though there is the most incredible prayer concerning divine healing help for spiritual warfare that was given to Pope Leo XIII. The story goes that after celebrating mass, the Pope had a distressing vision where he had been permitted to hear a conversation between God and the devil, and witness a disturbing scene of evil spirits trying to destroy the Church. However, he also saw the magnificent Archangel Michael appear and cast Satan and his legions into hell. It was because of this vision that the Pope composed the following prayer to Archangel Michael. I am including the shortened version here; the original version is much longer.

Archangel Michael Prayer (Shortened Version)

"Saint Michael the Archangel, defend us in battle; be our protection against the malice and snares of the devil. May God rebuke him we humbly pray; and do thou, O Prince of the Heavenly host, by the power of God, thrust into hell Satan and all the other evil spirits who wander through the world for the ruin of souls. Amen."

Use the prayer to help deliver you from all kinds of spiritual warfare, while also using the angel medicine exercises throughout the book to take charge of your energies.

Angel Medicine Exercise to Clear Your Mind, Body, and Soul of Spirit Attachments With Archangel Michael

Use this divine exercise to help you:

» Rid your energy of spirit attachments.

» Free your home from earthbound and low level spirits.

» Free yourself from the effects of fear.

» Overcome persistent headaches, skin complaints, and certain cravings/habits/attitudes.

» Move your body back into healing mode.

Time: approximately 2–3 minutes

Divine prayer

"I ask for the divine force and light of Archangel Michael to sweep through my home and my energy field to remove all spirit attachments and to free me from the effects of fear. I ask this in the name of God, Jesus Christ, and all that is Holy. Thank you, God. Thank you, Archangel Michael. Amen. It is done!"

Archangel power

Visualize yourself standing on a deep royal blue net of divine light that you are able to bend down and take hold of. Begin to pull this fine divine netting of light very slowly upward through your body, and just like a sieve will catch the lumps from any lumpy sauce you make, so will this fine netting catch any spirit attachments and discordant energies. (It is traveling through all of your subtle energy layers, where any spirit attachments and energetic anomalies may be located.) Take this fine divine netting way up above your head and imagine handing it to Archangel Michael, who will deal with any attachments and anomalies, and disperse any discordant energies. This very powerful divine exercise is an invaluable way to instantly clear your energy field.

Divine affirmation

"The divine light of Archangel Michael protects myself and my home."

Use this divine exercise daily and especially whenever you don't feel yourself or like something is amiss, or use it whenever you are fearful. You will soon notice how much more energized you begin to feel, and this extra energy will instantly help to serve your healing process.

Angel Medicine Exercise for Divine Protection With Archangel Michael

Use this divine exercise to help you:

» Protect your energy.

» Guard your mind.

» Improve your vitality.

» Free yourself from the effects of fear.

Time: approximately 2–3 minutes

Divine prayer

"I ask for divine protection from Archangel Michael to keep me safe from all harm, including any psychic or spiritual attack. I ask this in the name of God, Jesus Christ, and all that is Holy. Thank you, God. Thank you, Archangel Michael. Amen. It is done!"

Archangel power

Visualize pulling a deep royal blue cloak around you. This is the divine light and protective force of Archangel Michael. This magnificent blue cloak falls all the way to the ground, covering your feet. It also has a very large hood. Pull the hood over your head so that your body and head are completely covered. Wrap the cloak tightly around you and know that nothing other than divine love and light can now enter.

Energy healing technique

With either hand you are going to zip up your energy so that you remain unaffected by any detrimental unseen vibrations from other people, places, and spiritual forces. Move your hand to the area of your base energy center (pelvic area) and keep it held about 3 inches away from the body (not touching). Either pretend zipping up a cloak with your index finger or thumb, or use the flat palm of your hand to move your hand upward toward the top of your head and then into the air as far as you can stretch. Bring your hand back to the pelvic area, and do this exact same technique another two times. You will be drawing your energy field/pathway upward to help protect you by connecting your energies with the powers of heaven.

Divine affirmation

"The divine light of Archangel Michael protects my mind, body and soul."

Use this divine exercise daily and especially whenever you are fearful. You will soon notice how much more energized you begin to feel, and this extra energy will instantly help to serve your healing process.

Angel Surgeons

Another way to help those pesky health issues that continuously persist is to experience the divine healing process of angelic surgery. The impressive angelic surgeons can work deep within our energy field to help remove any energetic anomalies and seal any energy leaks that are detrimental to our health and happiness. Angelic surgery is a very powerful form of high-intensity and high-frequency divine restructuring and healing repair work, and all that is required from you to receive it are your imagination, your intention, and your openness toward it. The incredible angelic surgeons work under the direct guidance of the seven mighty and all-powerful Archangels. They perform specialized, intricate work within the higher subtle bodies of our bio-auric field, including the etheric template body.

The etheric template subtle body is associated to the fifth level of our aura, the throat energy center, and is the fifth subtle energy body. It provides the perfect holographic blueprint for the divine design of the lower etheric body. Our lower etheric body is nearest to the physical body, and is the energetic matrix and foundational support system for the physical body. (See Chapter 2.) The etheric template body appears to look like the negative of a photograph. The power and design behind the etheric template body are what maintain and enable the lower foundational etheric body to support the physical body's integrity and form.

Although we can make necessary changes to the lower etheric body ourselves to support our health, and you will soon discover exactly how to do so when you receive a fantastic etheric subtle body exercise, the fifth level subtle body energy work is best left to the divine celestial experts. It is an extremely powerful energy body to work with because it is the divine pattern of our perfect original blueprint of what God holds in divine mind concerning our physical body. This subtle body is perfect, and it will not require any actual changes other than within the energy field surrounding it so that its energy patterns can be realigned and reconnected with the physical etheric body.

When healing repairs are made at this level, they will reverberate throughout our entire auric field to pull all of our energies into their correct patterns. Divine restructuring work will especially help to support the lower etheric body and our physical health. Therefore, it is certainly best to allow the expert angelic surgeons to do the divine repair work.

Use the following specialized angel medicine exercise to allow the astonishing angelic surgeons to make any necessary divine healing repairs we may need.

Angel Medicine Angelic Surgery Exercise
Use this divine exercise to help you:

» Seal leaks and tears to regain instant vitality.

» Remove any energetic anomalies in our field.

» Repair any dysfunctions in our divine patterning found between our higher and lower etheric body.

» Restructure work (to help reconnect and realign with the body in its perfect state).

Time: approximately 5–10 minutes

Divine prayer

"I ask for the white light of the Holy Spirit to surround and protect my body and soul. Thank you, God. Amen. It is done!"

Angelic power

All that is required of you for this divine exercise are to maintain observation and witness the expert angelic surgeons go to work by using your imagination. They will repair any major energetic anomalies. They will seal and repair any subtle energy holes, remove any foreign etheric matter, and re-establish energetic power between the electrical templates. Let's begin!

Sit comfortably in a chair, and take a few long, slow, deep breaths and relax. Intend the following: *"I choose to focus on my etheric template energy body and energy field."* Begin to imagine an exact replica of your physical body standing in front of you. All you need to do is to hold this vision (simply maintain your imagination) for a few minutes while the angelic experts make any necessary alterations in your energy field in agreement with the will of God. This will enable them to perform intricate healing work. State the following divine request: *"I ask that any divine healing repairs needed to be made within my etheric template energy field be instantly made by the divine angelic surgeons in agreement with the will of God for my greatest and highest good. Thank you, God. Amen. It is done!"*

Immediately observe and witness any energetic changes taking place. This part of the process is extremely important because the very act of your observation will enable a divine healing repair to be instantly made. Imagine and intuitively sense the angel healing experts moving their hands over any parts of the energy field in need of repair, removing any foreign objects to be transmuted, and repairing any energy leaks and electrical dysfunctions. Remember: You are watching a scene of a replica you standing in front of you. You will intuitively know when the repairs have been completed and you are ready to finish. It can take anywhere from a few seconds to a few minutes to witness the healing work. Your act of witnessing and observing the repairs has ensured they have been corrected and altered. Finish by stating the following: *"Thank you, God. Thank you, divine angelic surgeons. Amen. It is done!"*

Etheric Subtle Body Healing

Finally, to finish this chapter you will be given an amazing angel medicine exercise that is focused on healing your etheric subtle energy body. This exercise is so wonderful that it can bring you instantaneous results in the way that you think and feel. It can help you to cope when you are totally overwhelmed. It can help you to feel alive and energized. It can help to place you back into healing mode. And it can help to clear inflammation and ease pain within the physical body. The results of this can be felt instantly or within hours of using it. The exercise I give you here is made easier for you than if you were using it in one of my workshops or courses. This is because much more intricate healing work can be performed within this fascinating subtle energy body that can be extremely beneficial to our health and well-being. However, I have definitely found that this shortened version of my original angel medicine exercise for subtle body healing works remarkably well.

Angel Medicine Exercise for Etheric Subtle Body Healing

Use this divine exercise to help you:

» Clear any compacted areas within your energy pathways or centers.

» Reduce energetic inflammation, and therefore physical inflammation.

» Repair any dysfunctional grid patterns and energy centers.

» Instantly clear the effects of emotional and mental stress.

» Instantly regain your vitality.

» Move your body back into healing mode.

Time: approximately 5–10 minutes

Divine prayer

"I ask for the white light of the Holy Spirit to surround and protect my body and soul. Thank you, God. Amen. It is done!"

Sit comfortably in a chair, and take a few long, slow, deep breaths and relax. Intend the following: *"I choose to focus on and repair any energetic issues within my etheric energy body for my greatest good."* Your higher self will present you with exactly what you can work on. Begin to imagine an exact replica of your physical body standing in front of you. Look directly at the top of the head and imagine turning on a pretend light switch so that your entire replica body lights up. The goal of this exercise is to quickly glimpse and see what areas *do not* light up.

Once you have quickly noticed what areas do not light up, you are then able to make the necessary changes through stating the following divine prayer and observing them happen. Look directly at the area needing to be altered and state: *"I ask that a divine healing change be made in this part of my body and be replaced with the correct, healthy vibration of my perfect original divine blueprint for my greatest good. Thank you, God. Amen. It is done!"*

Immediately observe and witness an energetic change taking place. This part of the process is extremely important because the very act of your observation will enable a divine healing change to be instantly made. You can do this by visualizing a smoky energy leaving the area that never lit up, and by visualizing intense bright white light being replaced in the area. Next, visualize your entire replica body glowing with vibrant orange light. Once this transformational stage is completed for all of the areas that you noticed were unlit, then your divine healing repairs are done. This can take seconds to witness. Your act of witnessing and observing the change has ensured it has been corrected and altered within you. Finish by stating the following: *"Thank you, God. Thank you, higher self. Amen. It is done!"*

Now that you have completed the deeper aspects of divine healing work it is time to understand more about how you can make greater use of your divine creative power and potential. Chapter 6 will introduce you to the astonishing process of divine celestial alchemy.

Chapter Six

Celestial Alchemists

Never give up on what you really want to do. The person with big dreams is more powerful than one with all the facts.

—Albert Einstein

I wonder how many people will skip through the book to read this appealing chapter first. The public interest in the ability to manifest our heart's desires is now mainstream due to the previous raging success of the book *The Secret,* and all other books that quickly followed suit in its genre. Manifesting is relatively easy because everyone *already* manifests according to their thoughts, beliefs, feelings, and expectations. We do this unconsciously all of the time, and so we often fail to acknowledge that what we see and have in our lives are either the happy or frustrating results of our very own creations. The art of manifestation becomes more powerful when we become conscious of what we desire to create—in other words, to become conscious participators in our own life stories, instead of just fanciful and wishful thinking with no action on our part. The art of manifesting at its greatest level, however, is achieved through the divine power of co-creation.

God's holy angels can and will help you in all your ways, and this exciting chapter will show you how you can join forces with the brilliantly creative celestial alchemists. You will be given a very powerful celestial alchemy formula, which you can then adapt to include and suit your own unique heartfelt desires. This stunningly powerful formula will immediately begin to initiate the process of co-creating with the highest forces of divine light. And who better to directly learn manifesting skills from than the actual angels of celestial alchemy. These impressive holy angels and divine teachers know exactly how to help you because part of their heavenly duties assist in overseeing and maintaining God's creation. They intimately know the divine laws of how to co-create with God. You are in for a very special divine treat!

The spiritual insight and celestial alchemy formula contained within this chapter can seriously improve and bless your life in the most wonderful, joyful, and fulfilling ways.

The Angels of Creation

The awe-inspiring angels of creation are responsible for overlooking and maintaining many different aspects of creation, under the will and direction of God. They are heavenly designers and highly evolved celestial beings of divine light who work with the very forces of creation to bring about divine results. Known as master creators and celestial alchemists, they have been imbued with the secret knowledge and wisdom of divine alchemy. Divine alchemy is not concerned with turning base metals into gold. Divine alchemy utilizes God's divine laws for us to co-create our lives in alignment with a higher power.

Divine alchemy will help us to transmute the lower aspects of our consciousness, so that we can turn our consciousness into the equivalent of spiritual Gold. We can then begin to shine brightly with our newly created spiritual power to help us effect wonderful and powerful life changes. We have the innate spiritual ability within our soul to co-design the most rewarding, joyful, and fulfilling life. It is now the perfect time in your life for you to rev up your divine creative potential and power!

Two Powerful Divine Laws From the Angels of Celestial Alchemy

1. Whatever you choose to co-create must always be in alignment with divine truth and divine love. This is for your own greatest and highest good, and to ensure that your manifesting work is divinely empowered and successful.

2. To achieve ever greater levels of success in your manifestations, whatever it is you choose to co-create, your intention must always be used in some unconditional way to be a divine blessing unto others. You are meant to add your own light to the world by passing along the goodwill, divine love, and blessings you co-create or receive from God, to help serve others. In doing so, you will keep the divine power of heaven flowing and ever increasing within your life.

*D*ivine Mergence

The miraculous angels of celestial alchemy want to reveal to you fascinating divine insight into how you can begin to co-create, manifest, and attract what you need and desire through divine mergence and by applying divine laws. Co-creation is your divine partnership with God, and this is certainly the greatest way in which you can begin to manifest your most fulfilling results. Conscious manifesting *without* God's alignment will still get you decent enough results because you do have a certain amount of limited creative power due to your free will. However, these results won't be as successful, as long lasting, or as fulfilling as you may hope them to be. Always include God in the use of your creative power to achieve the very best results. Your own power is limited until you decide to co-design with God, and then it becomes unlimited potential with infinite possibilities.

When we choose a higher power over our own limited creative power, we will actually merge our individual energy frequency with a holy divine force. Divine mergence also opens spiritual doors for us to receive God's grace. It is through the beautiful union of this holy divine mergence that begins to alter the very resonance of our energy frequency in the highest possible way. This will help to generate the immense divine power we require to help manifest our heartfelt desires into physical reality.

We need a combination of both divine light and energetic power to successfully manifest.

There are two significant and important ways to increase our spiritual power and our ability to successfully manifest:

» **Expand our consciousness through continuous spiritual growth.** The more light we hold within our soul, the greater our divine power and potential increase. Living in alignment with God's divine laws will naturally help us to expand our consciousness, increasing the divine light within our soul.

» **Looking after, balancing, and increasing our life force vitality**. When we are vitalized, we are physically, psychologically, and emotionally strong enough to empower the creativity of our soul. Our vitality is equivalent to a battery that can run down and be re-charged. We need to be fully charged to work without fault and for our soul power to shine through.

The following angel medicine exercise will help you to merge your consciousness with a higher divine power.

Angel Medicine Divine Mergence Exercise (Align with the divine powers of heaven)

Use this divine exercise to help you:

» Expand the divine light within your soul.

» Increase the spiritual power of your soul.

» Empower your manifestations.

Time: approximately 2 minutes

Divine prayer

"I ask that my own soul power blend with the seven powerful divine frequencies of God's holy Archangels so that this divine mergence will draw divine light, energy, and spiritual power into my being to help me in all my ways. I ask this in the name of God, Jesus Christ, and all that is Holy. Thank you, God. Thy will be done. Amen!"

Archangel power

Imagine your soul (consciousness) as a ball of white light (about the size of watermelon) and *you* as this ball of light are centered in your heart energy center. Move the ball of light in a straight line upward and out of your crown energy center to the golden sun of your higher self a few feet above your head. While it is here you will receive a portion of the seven frequencies of the divine light via the Archangels. Imagine your ball of light now changing into seven glorious colors of royal blue, golden yellow, rose pink, emerald green, sparkly white, purple/ ruby red, and violet so that your soul holds a beautiful rainbow of colors. You are now helping to imbue your soul with divine light, energy, and spiritual power. Bring the ball of light back to your heart energy center and settle your consciousness there. Imagine all of the colors emanating outward from your heart and filling your entire aura with these astonishing divine frequencies. That's it! Finish by stating the following: *"Thank you, God. Thank you, Archangels. Amen. It is done!"*

Divine Laws of Manifesting

Important divine laws and principles need to be taken into account for successful manifesting. Following are two of the most important, along with a wonderful angel medicine exercise to help you expand the radiant joy of your soul.

Only Heartfelt Dreams Count

Dreams that are not heart based and soul centered are simply dreams that come from the personality and ego. Such dreams include: *If only I had [more money, the right relationship a better job, more power and success, more talent], then I would be truly happy.* The soul knows this is a false truth that does not align with the highest divine forces. Until a person realizes that happiness is a personal choice, and is not connected or attached to anything that can be attained or achieved, then they will keep on searching for happiness *out there within the world,* instead of finding it within themselves.

Of course it is also true that wonderful relationships, family, good health, great friendships, fulfilling careers, abundance, and all other feel-good scenarios certainly add plenty to our inner happiness—but we are not meant to rely on anything outside of ourselves to keep us happy. Otherwise, if or when our worldly circumstances change, our happiness will be instantly gone. Our true, radiant joy comes from our divine heritage and from God. The divine truth is that being happy is completely related to the joy of our soul and our spiritual connection to God. *Happiness* is knowing that no matter what the unhappy circumstances of our life may presently be, when we place God first, those unhappy circumstances will only be temporary.

The following extremely powerful angel medicine exercise will help you blossom the radiant joy of your soul. You will be able to co-create, manifest, and attract to you all of your heartfelt desires and deepest dreams. It is one of the most potent divine exercises you can use to help you tap into your divine creative potential.

Angel Medicine Radiant Joy Exercise

Use this divine exercise to help you:

» Expand the divine light within your soul.

» Increase the creative spiritual power of your soul.

» Empower your manifestations.

» Increase your radiant joy in your life.

» Align with your divine origin.

Time: approximately 2 minutes

Divine prayer

"I ask that my soul truly remember its perfect divine origin and heritage within every cell of its spiritual DNA. I now recall my innate radiant joy back into my consciousness so that my spiritual creative power can bloom. I ask this for my greatest and highest good and the greatest good of all. Thank you, God. Thy will be done. Amen!"

Archangel power

This is a very symbolic exercise that requires the use of your imagination and visualization. You are going to open your very own imaginary pair of angel wings, as this imagery is highly symbolic of reawakening your innate spiritual power and radiance. Even though you are using your imagination, you are absolutely working with very important energy frequencies to make some wonderful energetic changes. Let's begin!

Place your awareness on the area between your shoulder blades at the back of your body. In doing this you are centering your soul consciousness there. Just notice what you feel while you are observing this area. The back of the heart energy center is connected to your deservedness and to your actual alignment with your deepest dreams. When you work with the energy frequencies of this center your dreams can start to become a reality instead of just a dream.

When you are ready, state the following request to show you are ready to open your own symbolic set of angel wings: *"I am ready to accept all goodness within my life and to align with my deepest dreams so that they become part of my physical life experience."*

Now imagine that you are opening your own set of angel wings. With your creative imagination, allow these wings to open fully and spread out wide. Your opening wings are helping you to reawaken your innate creative power, which is related to your radiant joy, so you can bring your dreams into reality. Do you feel any tingling, any heat, any area of tickling, itching, or even slight pain, but not pain in any severe way? You may notice nothing at all. If you do, it is just a tangible sign that you are working on your energy frequencies. However, it really doesn't matter if you don't. Just go with the exercise and finish when you feel you have fully opened your wings.

Energy healing technique

On a lesser energetic level, your radiant joy is also concerned with your sacral energy center and emotional subtle body. To help your radiant joy blossom and your creativity bloom, you can help to energize, re-balance, and realign the energy center and the subtle body. Place your right hand directly and lightly on the area below your navel, and your left hand on your lower back in direct alignment with the right one (in a position you find comfortable). Divine light and subtle energies will begin to be drawn to this area. Keep your hands in this position for a few minutes while you simply imagine pure white light filling the space between your hands. After a few minutes remove your hands and shake them away from you, down toward the ground to release any excess energies. That's it! Finish by stating the following: *"Thank you, God. Amen. It is done!"*

You will soon notice subtle to profound shifts happening within your life because the radiant joy of your soul is able to blossom.

*T*he Divine Law of Attraction

The divine law of attraction concerns the quality of our consciousness, and the conscious or unconscious energy we give out to the world. What we give out, we will draw back toward us. It is a typical cause and effect situation that works hand-in-hand with the free will God gave us to create our lives. If we are unforgiving, mean-spirited, cold-hearted, jealous of others, and self-serving, then our inner consciousness that we express outward to the world will be severely out of alignment with divine truth and divine love (unenlightened). Also, our energy vibration will also hold a very low, slow, and dense heavy frequency.

This dense frequency, due to our consciousness, determines our current level and point of attraction. We will then begin to attract back to us the annoying results of our own mind—the limiting return of our own thoughts, beliefs, and actions. Plus, what we truly dream of having, we will also unwittingly repel with our energy frequency— and therefore push our heartfelt desires firmly out of bounds because we do not have enough light or spiritual power within our soul to create and attract it.

The good news is that this disruption can be instantly altered any time you are willing to correct the initial interfering cause and energetic pattern. Use the angel medicine exercises found within Chapter 4 and Chapter 5 to help you correct and alter anything destructive within your consciousness if you find you continuously experience problems with co-creating your heartfelt dreams and desires. Oftentimes we do not realize that we hold deep resentments, jealousies, hatred, and other low-vibrational frequencies within our consciousness because we believe we are basically good. Being spiritual requires more than being good. It requires that we live our truth in alignment with God's divine truth and divine love. Here are two powerful divine secrets to help encourage you in your manifesting work to keep expanding the divine light within your soul, so that you can co-create with the powers of heaven:

» Do your best to recognize, and become energetically responsible for and spiritually mature of where you need to receive divine correction. You must recognize your need for divine correction and you must want it, ask for divine help, correct it, and then you must continue to move forward heavenward. (You can use the exercises found within this book to do so.)

» Do your best to think, speak, and act in alignment with divine truth and divine love. This is how you unconditionally give back to the world; you *become* a vehicle for the light of God within you to be expressed to the world.

That's it. Hooray! It is now time to begin co-creating through the divine power of celestial alchemy.

*C*elestial Alchemy
Miracles Can and Do Happen

God has placed a special dream within your heart, and if you can dream it, then you can achieve it. Nothing is too big, too difficult, or too impossible for you to co-create, manifest, or attract that you deeply dream of. God can open doors for you that no man has yet opened. God is not bothered by your earthly credentials to take you places, as He is more concerned with your soul's credentials, and He knows that you have exactly what it takes. You are being blessed from all directions right now, so prepare to shine. This is your time now.

How to Co-Design Your Own Miracles

It is now time to get down to the nitty-gritty of divine manifesting. The angel medicine celestial alchemy formula is typically the same format for all of your manifesting needs, only requiring a few tweaks and adjustments here and there, so that it can be especially adapted for what it is you truly desire. First read through the formula's principles and example to help familiarize yourself with the process, and then you will discover a few planned formulas for you that have been especially adapted for some of our most natural human desires. Use them as a guide to be totally creative with any specific manifestations you wish to divinely design for yourself. Let's begin!

$\mathcal{A}$ngel Medicine Celestial Alchemy Formula: Principles and Example

Principle One: Ask the Angels

Always begin by asking for divine help: *"Angels of celestial alchemy, I ask that you help me to bring my heartfelt dreams and desires (be specific) into reality for my greatest and highest good, and for the greatest good of all. Thank you, God. Thank you, angels. Amen. It is done!"* Asking ensures you are co-designing with the powers of heaven and are not going it all alone.

Principle Two: Make Energetic Space

Clear plenty of energetic space for what you desire. Always focus on the end result of your dream. Begin to think, feel, and act from this end result. As an example, let's say you've asked for help in attracting true unconditional love into your life. You must now begin to make energetic space for that love by clearing out any interfering energies that can cause conflict with your dreams. Clear some energetic space mentally, emotionally, and physically as follows:

To clear some mental space: Begin to monitor your thoughts and beliefs about your heartfelt dream so that you keep your focus on your end result, and not centered on what is currently missing or lacking within your life. Going along with the same example of attracting true love, imagine and visualize yourself spending time with an amazing partner—one who is caring, honest, sincere, unconditionally loving, supportive, spiritual, and the list can go on. Think of the wonderful conversations you will both share with each other. *Do this process for a few minutes two to three times a day.*

Keep your thoughts clear from the likes of "I am lonely, I wish I had someone to love me, I will never get married, and I am unlucky in love." They will only serve to block and hinder true love from entering. These thoughts will also reveal your core limiting beliefs that will need to be corrected and realigned with divine truth and divine love. (You can use the divine exercises found within this book to do so. Also use the divine declaration and gratitude affirmation further along this celestial alchemy formula to help you.)

To clear some emotional space: Let go of all past hurts and open your heart fully toward attracting new love. You must be willing to trust in love with no guarantees of success for your heart to be fully opened. This ensures that you are not attached to love or attempting to control the conditions of love in any way. Love is free, and it needs to be given and received freely without condition. (You can use the divine exercises found within this book to help you heal any past hurts that have blocked your heart energy.)

Begin to *really feel* how happy, fulfilled, and wonderful it is to be in love with this fantastic new partner of yours. (Using your emotions to help you is one of the most powerful tools you can utilize.) When you combine the emotional power of *feeling* into your imagination, visualization, and divine declaration work, you have the most spectacular soul recipe for success. *Do this process for a few minutes two to three times a day.*

To clear some physical space: Use some physical actions so you can begin to design your house and environment ready and in great expectation for a wonderful new partner to share your life with. Clear out wardrobe space, and set an extra place setting at the dinner table. Begin to act as if you are already sharing your home with the perfect person for you. You know what to do; be creative.

Principle Three: Declare Your Divine Origin

Use a divine declaration and gratitude affirmation: *"I have true love in my life because unconditional love is my true divine origin. Thank you, God, for my true love."* You can repeat this divine declaration throughout the day.

Principle Four: Divine Timing

Let go, and let God and His holy angels deal with your dream in divine timing, while you keep your heart energy fully open.

Celestial Alchemy Formula for Abundance
Principle One: Ask the Angels

"Angels of celestial alchemy, I ask that you help me to become abundant and bring my heartfelt dream and desire of abundance into reality for my greatest and highest good, and for the greatest good of all. Thank you, God. Thank you, angels. Amen. It is done!"

Principle Two: Make Energetic Space

To clear mental space: Begin to align your thoughts, beliefs, visualizations, and imagination with being abundant. How would you think and what would you believe if you were truly abundant? Example: *"All of my needs are continuously met. I have God's blessings and favor in my life. I am so blessed. I am so happy. I am very creative. I am successful. I am abundant."* Begin to imagine and visualize yourself being abundant. What would you do if you had no financial limitations, for instance? Let your imagination be your guide. *Do this process for a few minutes two to three times a day.* (You can use the divine exercises within this book for any thoughts, beliefs, and behaviors that need to be corrected and realigned with divine truth and divine love.)

To clear emotional space: Utilize the power of your emotions to truly feel abundant. How would you feel if you were truly abundant? Here are a few examples: happy, radiant, fulfilled, free, safe, secure, successful, joyous, happy because you can be a blessing to others, and the list goes on. It is the *feeling* component of your dream that is the most important aspect of your celestial alchemy formula. *Do this process for a few minutes two to three times a day.*

To clear physical space: Use some physical actions to give to others. You can give a gift to charity, give your time, give your unconditional love and support to another in need, give your talent, give your radiant joy to the world, and give your prayers for others. Just keep your heart energy open to give, give, and give, while also remaining open to receiving. Be creative!

Principle Three: Declare Your Divine Origin

"I have abundance in my life because abundance is my true divine origin. Thank you, God, for my abundance." You can repeat this divine declaration throughout the day.

Principle Four: Divine Timing

Let go, and let God and His holy angels deal with your dream in divine timing, while you keep your heart energy fully open.

Special Information About Acquiring Abundance

The opposite of abundance is lack. Therefore to create abundance in your life you need to take your focus off what is missing in your life, what you lack in your life, and what you don't have and don't want in your life. To achieve abundance it is very important to focus on what true abundance divinely represents. True abundance is an aspect of God's divine love and power, as well as an aspect of your true divine nature. You are made in the image and likeness of God. When you claim your divine heritage and you recognize the true source of your abundance, you will continuously increase your abundant soul energy and expand the flow of giving and receiving within your life.

By choosing to develop an abundant energy vibration, you will begin to draw to you golden opportunities sent by the powers of heaven, to keep advancing your level and potential of abundance. You will get that unexpected pay raise, you will be promoted when you didn't even expect to be, you will be offered that new job, and you will be open to receive God's abundance, blessings, and favor in your life. This is much more remarkable than any singular desire to receive a certain amount of money. Money is only one small outward stream and expression of true divine abundance.

Celestial Alchemy Formula for True Happiness (The Secret of Longevity and All Blessings) Principle One: Ask the Angels

"Angels of celestial alchemy, I ask that you help me to become and experience my heartfelt dream and desire of true happiness

for my greatest and highest good, and for the greatest good of all. Thank you, God. Thank you, angels. Amen. It is done!"

Principle Two: Make Energetic Space

To clear mental space: Align your thoughts, beliefs, visualizations, and imagination with being happy. How would you think and what would you believe if you were truly happy? Example: *"I love and accept myself, I love my life, I know who I am in God, I love my family and friends, I love humanity, I am loving, I am caring, and I create joy through my own uniqueness."* Begin to imagine and visualize yourself being truly happy. What would you do if you had no limitations holding you back, for instance? Let your imagination be your guide. *Do this process for a few minutes two to three times a day.* (You can use the divine exercises within this book for any thoughts, beliefs, and behaviors that need to be corrected and realigned with divine truth and divine love.)

To clear emotional space: Utilize the power of your emotions to truly feel happy. How would you feel if you were truly happy? Here are a few examples: radiantly happy, fulfilled, free from fear, safe, secure, peaceful, joyous, and the list goes on. It is the *feeling* component of your dream that is the most important aspect of your celestial alchemy formula. *Do this process for a few minutes two to three times a day.*

To clear physical space: Use some physical actions to create your happiness. Align your actions with your heart's deepest desires, and this will lead toward you expressing and living your truth. De-clutter what no longer serves your greatest good from your life and your environment. Make someone you care about happy. Make a stranger happy. Be your true self and spread your radiant joy to the world. Use your unique gifts and talents to bring joy and happiness to others. This is your life purpose, and it will help to shine the light of your soul. Be creative!

Principle Three: Declare Your Divine Origin

"I have true happiness in my life because happiness and radiant joy are my true divine origin. Thank you, God, for my happiness and radiant joy." You can repeat this divine declaration throughout the day.

Principle Four: Divine Timing

Let go, and let God and His holy angels deal with your dream in divine timing while you keep your heart energy fully open.

The secret of happiness is to bring happiness to others through being you. Never wish to be someone else, as you are perfect being you. When you realize this you can use your own uniqueness to shine. Appreciate and enjoy other people's natural talents for who they are, as we are all made to be different for a reason. Share your radiant joy and specialty with the world, and you will become fulfilled in doing so. God made you, *you* for a reason and a divine purpose. Love yourself, love your life, be true to yourself, and be happy.

Happy manifesting!
Have fun and remember to radiate your joy.

Afterword

Angel Medicine for Preventive Care

Fantastic! You have finished reading *The Power of Angel Medicine,* and now you will hopefully understand just how important and beneficial it really is to take responsibility for your own portion of divine energies. You can truly help yourself whenever you willingly choose to align with the divine, so start celebrating your newfound energetic power today! Let the phrase *align with the divine* become your new spiritual mantra. Remember: God's holy angels are only a thought away, and they are always ready to help you with any health challenges and life complaints you may be experiencing. All you ever need to do is to ask!

You can refer back to this book as a helpful guide and point of reference should the need arise for any specific issues that may present themselves in the future. You can also use the angel medicine exercises within this book to directly help and inspire your loved ones, friends, or clients whenever *they* are going through any kind of energy blips or frustrating obstacles.

I am delighted to leave you with an impressive combination of five specially selected angel medicine exercises and energetic techniques, exclusively designed to help you achieve a good level of daily spiritual and energetic self-care. The daily use of these five easy-to-use and quick-to-perform divinely inspired exercises can help to create instant balance and flow among your energy fields, systems, pathways, and subtle frequencies. They will enable you to quickly restore your energetic power and stabilize your entire vibrational frequency. Daily care of your energy in this way will serve you well in the long run as you will remain vitalized and empowered to stay in healing mode. Here are the final five angel medicine exercises and energetic techniques for your daily self-care:

Angel Medicine Divine Protection Exercise

Use this divine exercise to help you:

» Establish divine spiritual protection.

» Protect your vitality.

» Keep you in healing mode.

Time: approximately 1 minute

Divine prayer

"I ask for the white light of the Holy Spirit and the divine force of Archangel Michael to surround and protect my body and soul. Thank you, God. Amen. It is done!"

Archangel power

Visualize pulling a deep royal blue cloak around you. This is the divine light and protective force of Archangel Michael. This magnificent blue cloak falls all the way to the ground, covering your feet. It also has a very large hood. Pull the hood over your head so that your body and head are completely covered. Wrap the cloak tightly around you, and know that nothing other than divine love and light can now enter.

Divine affirmation: *"The divine light of Archangel Michael protects my body and soul."*

Angel Medicine "Unscramble Your Energies" Technique

Use this divine exercise to help you:

» Improve your energetic circulation.

» Balance your energies.

» Improve your coordination.

» Protect your vitality.

» Keep you in healing mode.

Time: approximately 2 minutes

Healing Points

Use your index, middle, and ring fingertips to massage or tap the acupressure points known as the K-27 points, with moderate pressure, and with your arms crossed over each other. They are paired energy points located on both sides of the body found just below the collarbone in the small indentations. Take a few long, slow, deep breaths as you massage or tap them, and relax. Do this for about 30 seconds.

Next, with the middle fingertip of your right hand gently hold (very light pressure) the brow energy center point located between and a little above the eyebrows. This potent technique can help to clear mental fatigue, confusion, and irritability. Hold for one minute and then finish.

Next, touch your left knee or ankle with your right hand, and then touch your right knee or ankle with your left hand. Now touch your left shoulder with your right hand, and then touch your right shoulder with your left hand. This will take you a few seconds to do. And then finish. You are helping to positively influence the energetic patterns concerned with both hemispheres of the brain.

Angel Medicine "Align With the Divine" Exercise

Use this divine exercise to help you:

» Align with the divine.

» Protect your vitality.

» Keep you in healing mode.

Time: approximately 2 minutes

Divine prayer

Dear God, please work within my body, mind, soul, and life for my greatest good. I love you, God. I love my life. Thank you, God."

This is an extremely powerful prayer that will help you to develop your personal relationship with God through opening your heart and soul to the divine power.

"Align with the divine" exercise

Begin with your hands in prayer position held over the center of your chest area. Take a few long, slow, deep breaths in through the nose and out of the mouth, and relax. Next, stretch one arm up toward the heavens with your palm facing heavenward, while your other arm moves down to your side with your palm facing the ground. You will begin to draw divine light and subtle energies from both heaven and earth (balancing your energies) into your palms. You can even visualize white light pouring in through your palm stretched above your head, and vibrant orange light pouring in to your palm facing the ground. After a minute of doing this, bring your hands back into prayer position and hold them over the center of your chest. That's it.

Divine affirmation: *"I am aligned with the divine powers of heaven."*

Angel Medicine "Tap in Your Joy" Technique

Use this divine exercise to help you:

» Increase your radiant joy.

» Create positive new habits.

» Empower your creativity.

» Keep you in healing mode.

Time: approximately 1 minute

Healing Points

Use the index, middle, and ring fingertips of your left hand to place them lightly on the center of your chest area (bony part). Keep them there as you use the middle fingertip of your right hand to gently hold (very light pressure) the brow energy center point located between and a little above the eyebrows. Stay this way for a one minute as you help to balance and realign the energies of your heart to your head. With a very gentle tapping motion, tap the area of your brow energy center point while you repeat the following statement three times: *"I am radiantly happy."* That's it.

Angel Medicine Pain-Relief Technique

Use this divine exercise to help you:

» Ease and relieve pain.

» Boost your vitality.

» Keep you in healing mode.

Time: approximately 1 minute

Healing Points

With your index, middle, and ring fingertips of both hands, lightly hold the healing points located at the lower back of your head in the indentations where the ridge of your skull meets your neck. Take a few long, slow, deep breaths in through the nose and out of the mouth, and relax. You may feel a warm, burning-like, or hot sensation in your fingertips as you continue to hold these points. This is a good sign, as your energies will be connecting. You will also help to draw divine light and subtle energies to where they are most needed. Stay like this for one minute.

~9)

Author's Message

*J*ust for You!

I have fulfilled one of my own heartfelt dreams in writing this book, which would not have come about without my divine alignment to God through His holy angels. It is therefore my sincere hope that the divine healing power contained within this book will instantly touch your heart and soul, light up your life, and help to encourage you to fulfill your own deepest dreams and healing. You are an exquisite and beautiful soul who is imbued with the divine spark of God. Divine love is the very essence of your being. When you realize this beautiful divine truth, you will also realize that you are not meant to struggle, but you are meant to soar. And you will gain the spiritual freedom and the divine power you need to create and attract the most wonderful, healthy, happy, and radiant life.

In divine love and with angel blessings,
Joanne Brocas

Index

About the Author

Joanne Brocas is a professionally trained medium, angel expert, intuitive healer, Reiki Master/teacher, and bestselling author with more than two decades of experience in afterlife communication and healing. During her childhood, Joanne communicated with her guardian angel and has maintained a very strong, clear connection with the Spirit World and angelic realm throughout her life. Joanne is the founder of Chakra Medicine School of Energy Healing and Intuitive Development, helping to teach others how to develop their intuitive awareness, how to connect to the angels, and how to ignite their own healing power. Born in South Wales, UK, Joanne now lives in Orlando, Florida, with her husband and teaches board-approved healing programs and workshops nationally.

To find out more about Joanne and her angel medicine healing work, online courses, and workshops, you can visit her Websites: *www.chakramedicine.com* and *www.joannebrocas.com*.